PARTY LOYALTY
AMONG
CONGRESSMEN

THE DIFFERENCE BETWEEN DEMOCRATS
AND REPUBLICANS · 1947–1962

DAVID R. MAYHEW

HARVARD UNIVERSITY PRESS
CAMBRIDGE · MASSACHUSETTS · 1966

© 1966 by the President and Fellows of Harvard College
All rights reserved
Distributed in Great Britain by Oxford University Press, London
Publication of this book has been aided by a grant from the Ford Foundation
Library of Congress Catalog Card Number 66-21341
Printed in the United States of America

TO MY PARENTS

ACKNOWLEDGMENTS

MOST IMPORTANT to me in the writing of this work were the genius and the generosity of the late V. O. Key, Jr.; Professor Key gave me both inspiration and direction. Others who read the chapters at an early stage and provided helpful criticism were Joseph Cooper, Milton C. Cummings, Jr., Samuel P. Huntington, H. Douglas Price, and Paul Shupack. I take full responsibility, of course, for the product in its final form. During the time of most intensive writing I was sustained in part by funds from the Frank G. Thomson Bequest.

David R. Mayhew

Amherst, Massachusetts
Spring 1966

CONTENTS

TABLES

FIGURES

PARTY LOYALTY AMONG CONGRESSMEN

1/INTRODUCTION

"[A]ll this talk about caucus is just a dream anyway. The Democrats are so deeply split in philosophy that they cannot encourage anything which might divide them even more."
— AN UNIDENTIFIED DEMOCRATIC CONGRESSMAN[1]

"And in the third place, when Senator X or Senator Z does something I think is just deplorable, more than half the time that means he's a Republican— *supposed* to be helping me, not working against me."
— PRESIDENT DWIGHT D. EISENHOWER[2]

OF WHAT IMPORTANCE is party affiliation in the United States Congress? One way to find out is to examine the voting records of congressmen; accordingly, students of government have long thought congressional voting a fitting object of their attentions. Unusual powers would be needed to discover consistency or order in the directing of these attentions, for American political science has changed more in the last half century than the Congress itself. The profession has been converted from a subdivision of history into a subdivision of sociology, and it is fast becoming a subdivision of mathematics. Studies of congressional voting behavior reflect the trend. The chasm separating A. Lawrence Lowell's 1901 work, "The Influence of Party Upon Legislation in England and America," [3] from

1. Quoted in Charles L. Clapp, *The Congressman: His Work as He Sees It* (Washington, D.C., 1963), p. 299.
2. Quoted in Emmet John Hughes, *The Ordeal of Power: A Political Memoir of the Eisenhower Years* (New York, 1963), p. 124.
3. *Annual Report of the American Historical Association for 1901*, I, 319–542 (reprinted Washington, D.C., 1902).

a more recent study such as R. Duncan Luce's and Arnold A. Rogow's "A Game Theoretic Analysis of Congressional Power Distributions for a Stable Two-Party System" [4] is a wide one indeed. In political science, as in other matters, whether evolution denotes progress or not is an unsettled question.

The historian is inevitably concerned with the unique. Thus political scientists of a historical bent have used congressional voting data to throw light on particular historical problems. Lowell, in his analysis of Parliament and Congress, marshaled quantitative data to establish a contrast between British and American party operations and to detect historical trends in the legislative practices of each country. V. O. Key, Jr., in *Southern Politics in State and Nation*,[5] used congressional roll call data in examining the status of the one-party South in national politics. Julius Turner, in *Party and Constituency: Pressures on Congress*,[6] explored shifting party alignments in Congress by analyzing roll call figures from four Congresses ranging from the Sixty-seventh to the Seventy-eighth. Robert A. Dahl and others interested in the development and sustenance of American foreign policy have found valuable information in the voting records of senators and congressmen.[7] Over among the historians, Howard W. Allen has recently used congressional roll calls to locate the geographical basis of Progressive sentiment in the Wilson era.[8]

4. *Behavioral Science,* 1:83–95 (April 1956).
5. (New York, 1949), chaps. xvi–xvii.
6. (Baltimore, 1951).
7. Robert A. Dahl, *Congress and Foreign Policy* (New York, 1950); George L. Grassmuck, *Sectional Biases in Congress on Foreign Policy* (Baltimore, 1951); H. Bradford Westerfield, *Foreign Policy and Party Politics: Pearl Harbor to Korea* (New Haven, 1955); Malcolm E. Jewell, *Senatorial Politics and Foreign Policy* (Lexington, Ky., 1962); Leroy N. Rieselbach, "The Demography of the Congressional Vote on Foreign Aid, 1939–1958," *American Political Science Review,* 58:577–588 (September 1964).
8. "Geography and Politics: Voting on Reform Issues in the United

The authors of the foregoing studies have employed congressional voting statistics to examine historical situations. Of late, however, the field of congressional voting has been staked out by behavioral scientists. Scholars of the behavioral persuasion have analyzed voting data with the object of formulating nonhistorical propositions about congressional or legislative behavior — and of contributing to the building of a comprehensive science of politics. David B. Truman's excellent 1959 work, *The Congressional Party: A Case Study*,[9] differs in focus from Turner's study of a decade before; Truman, only marginally interested in policy questions, could extract from the records of a single Congress the kinds of behavioral information he sought. In many recent discussions of legislative voting (not all of them by political scientists), a concern with methodological refinement has been accompanied by a diminishing interest in the study of historical events.[10] In the latest works applying mathematics to legislative voting,

---

States Senate, 1911–1916," *Journal of Southern History*, 27:216–228 (May 1961).

9. (New York, 1959).

10. Postwar works on methodology include Chester W. Harris, "A Factor Analysis of Selected Senate Roll Calls, 80th Congress," *Educational and Psychological Measurement*, 8:583–591 (Winter 1948); N. L. Gage and Ben Shimberg, "Measuring Senatorial 'Progressivism,'" *Journal of Abnormal and Social Psychology*, 44:112–117 (January 1949); Duncan MacRae, Jr., "Some Underlying Variables in Legislative Roll Call Votes," *Public Opinion Quarterly*, 18:191–196 (Summer 1954); George M. Belknap, "A Method for Analyzing Legislative Behavior," *Midwest Journal of Political Science*, 2:377–402 (November 1958); Charles D. Farris, "A Method of Determining Ideological Groupings in the Congress," *Journal of Politics*, 20:308–338 (May 1958); Paul Dempsey, "Liberalism-Conservatism and Party Loyalty in the U.S. Senate," *Journal of Social Psychology*, 56:159–170 (April 1962); John G. Grumm, "A Factor Analysis of Legislative Behavior," *Midwest Journal of Political Science*, 7:336–356 (November 1963). Two influential methodological works of earlier years are Stuart A. Rice, *Quantitative Methods in Politics* (New York, 1928), and Herman C. Beyle, *Identification and Analysis of Attribute-Cluster-Blocs* (Chicago, 1931).

the detachment of political science from history is almost complete.[11]

The study presented in the following pages can perhaps best be described as a historical essay. The subject of concern is the manner in which the congressional parties operated in handling certain domestic political issues in a given historical period. No corollary conclusions are drawn about congressional behavior in any other era of history. The span of years chosen for scrutiny is the sixteen-year period extending from 1947 to 1962, from the opening of the Eightieth Congress to the close of the Eighty-seventh.

A number of reasons underlie the selection of these particular years. There are two considerations of convenience. Roll call data for all postwar Congresses are available in presentable form; *Congressional Quarterly* offers voting breakdowns by party and by state. In addition, since the study requires that congressional districts be treated as continuous historical units there is also the problem of revisions in district boundaries. Most districts survived (at least in recognizable form) the changes provoked by the 1950 Census, but few could endure the orgy of redistricting touched off by the 1960 Census and the subsequent reapportionment decisions of the Supreme Court. The Eighty-seventh Congress, elected in 1960, was the last to serve the old constituencies.

The choice of this span of years rests, however, upon logic

11. See Luce and Rogow, "A Game Theoretic Analysis"; William H. Riker, "The Paradox of Voting and Congressional Rules for Voting on Amendments," *American Political Science Review,* 52:349–366 (June 1958); Duncan MacRae, Jr. and Hugh D. Price, "Scale Positions and 'Power' in the Senate," *Behavioral Science,* 4:212–218 (July 1959); William H. Riker, "A Method for Determining the Significance of Roll Calls in Voting Bodies," in John C. Wahlke and Heinz Eulau, eds., *Legislative Behavior: A Reader in Theory and Research* (Glencoe, Ill., 1959), pp. 377–384; William H. Riker and Donald Niemi, "The Stability of Coalitions on Roll Calls in the House of Representatives," *American Political Science Review,* 56:58–65 (March 1962).

as well as convenience. The fact that each party held the Presidency for eight of the sixteen years lends the period an appropriate partisan balance. More important, an argument can be made that, despite the presidential turnover, this postwar period was one of considerable issue stability; a 1962 legislator transported back to the Eightieth Congress would have found that body wrestling with many rather familiar domestic problems. A further argument can be made that the period was one of impressive stability in political alignments. By 1946 Congress had felt the full impact of the New Deal electoral revolution; the all but complete disappearance from Congress of Midwestern Republican progressives and Northern Democratic conservatives had already elevated each party to a new and quite stable level of ideological purity. By 1962 there were new signs of change; political turbulence in the South was fast eroding away some of the landmarks of postwar congressional politics. The 1947–1962 period is, in short, one for which congressional voting figures are easily accessible and one which can be treated with some justification as a discrete historical unit.

The object will be to analyze extensively the operations of each party in the postwar House of Representatives in dealing with farm issues, with city issues, with labor issues, and with Western issues. Because the House has more than four times as many members as the Senate, statistical findings about its transactions can be put forth in greater detail and with greater confidence. The choice of the four stated sets of domestic issues for examination is dictated by the choice of methodology to be used in examining them. Legislation affecting the farmer, the city dweller, the worker, or the Westerner can be presumed to be of special concern to an identifiable minority of congressmen from "interested" districts. In each case, the "interested" minority in these postwar years included congressmen

of both parties. For each set of issues, clues about party operations will be sought in an analysis of the relations prevailing
between "interested" and relatively "indifferent" wings of each
party in roll call votes on issues of presumed concern to the
"interested" congressmen. Thus no attention will be devoted
to issues such as foreign aid or social security which did not
clearly concern or affect some House constituencies more than
others. Of all the congressional battles of this postwar era,
however, a sizable proportion were fought over the four kinds
of "bread and butter" issues to be discussed here. (Civil rights,
though a district issue, will not be covered. Because everyone
knew that the Senate was in fact the resolving body in this
period, there was always a certain unreality in House treatment
of civil rights questions.)

The selection of House roll call votes for examination has
been an entirely arbitrary undertaking. From the records of
the postwar period, 110 roll calls have been chosen as "farm
votes," 51 as "city votes," 56 as "labor votes," and 92 as
"Western votes." Roll calls have been included in each of the
four issue sets if they were on matters thought to be of special
concern to the identifiable "interested" minorities of congressmen. Thus a roll call on feed grains legislation is classified as
a "farm vote," a roll call on public housing a "city vote," a
roll call on minimum wage revision a "labor vote," and a roll
call on reclamation policy a "Western vote." In some cases,
several votes on various aspects of the same legislation have
been included. No roll calls have been counted on which 90
percent or more of all recorded congressmen voted on the same
side of a question; the effect is to limit the discussion to issues
about which there was a modicum of controversy. No special
treatment has been given to "party votes." [12] Finally, no at-

12. "Party votes" have been variously defined. Lowell, in "The Influence of Party Upon Legislation in England and America," defined a

tempt has been made to "weight" the votes, to assign some issues more importance than others. All the roll calls in each issue set are treated as mathematical equals, the goal being the inclusion of as many votes as possible and the assumption being that there exists no objective means of ranking votes according to their significance.[13] Except where they are divided, for purposes of demonstration, into groups of votes recorded in each separate postwar Congress, all the roll calls in each of the four issues sets will be dealt with as a homogeneous block.

The argument in the following chapters rests on the assumption that congressmen can be identified whose constituencies compel a solicitude for certain policies and programs. Thus, the reasoning goes, a Colorado congressman can be expected to approve of dams, and a North Dakota congressman must

---

"party vote" of any *one* party as a roll call on which more than 90 percent of recorded members of the party vote on the same side of a question. Westerfield, in *Foreign Policy and Party Politics,* defined a "party-line vote" as a roll call on which simple majorities of *both* parties oppose each other. Dempsey, in "Liberalism-Conservatism and Party Loyalty in the U.S. Senate," argues persuasively that the ideological positions of senators are less apparent on "party-line votes" (using the Westerfield definition) than on roll calls where majorities of both parties are in agreement; the tightening of party lines draws liberal Republicans to the right and conservative Democrats to the left.

13. Riker, in "A Method for Determining the Significance of Roll Calls in Voting Bodies," has suggested an interesting way of ranking roll calls according to the significance given to them by legislators at the time of voting. The proposition is that significance varies with both narrowness of outcome and proportion of legislators voting. Thus a house roll call of greatest significance would be one with a 218–217 outcome, a roll call of least significance one with a 218–0 outcome (218 is a quorum). This suggestion may prove to be useful. One note of skepticism should be voiced; Riker applied the method to the Senate roll calls of the Eighty-third Congress and found — as the mathematics would dictate — that the roll call on the McCarthy censure was not of major significance. The problem is that roll calls are used not only to register the outcomes of struggles for victory, but also to record simple demonstrations of allegiance; to identify "significance" with the former use may be a bit Procrustean.

display an interest in sustaining the price of wheat. To match the four selected sets of issues, four sets of congressional districts have been chosen in which the issues are presumed to have been of political salience in this postwar period. Relevant indices have been used to delineate "farm districts," "city districts," and "labor districts"; "Western districts" have been taken to include all districts in the Mountain and Pacific states. (That is, Arizona, California, Colorado, Idaho, Montana, Nevada, New Mexico, Oregon, Utah, Washington, Wyoming, and, eventually, Alaska and Hawaii.) In the Eighty-seventh Congress, there were 111 congressmen from "farm districts," 140 from "city districts," 129 from "labor districts," and 59 from "Western districts." In some cases the categories overlapped; the Fifth California district (San Francisco), for example, was counted as a "Western district," as a "labor district," and as a "city district."

Recent studies pointing to a lack of awareness among constituents of their congressmen's policy positions suggest that "constituency pressure" on particular issues is not as potent as it was once believed to be.[14] It is assumed here, however, that some logical relationship ordinarily exists between the public positions of congressmen and the demographic characteristics of their districts, whether the connection derives from the pressures of constituents few or many, from congressmen's perceptions of their constituents' needs and demands, or from the workings of the congressional nomination process.

Isolation of the four sets of "interested" districts makes pos-

14. See Thomas V. Gilpatrick, "Price Support Policy and the Midwest Farm Vote," *Midwest Journal of Political Science,* 3:319–335 (November 1959); Donald E. Stokes and Warren E. Miller, "Party Government and the Saliency of Congress," *Public Opinion Quarterly,* 26:531–546 (Winter 1962); Warren E. Miller and Donald E. Stokes, "Constituency Influence in Congress," *American Political Science Review,* 57:45–56 (March 1963); V. O. Key, Jr., *Public Opinion and American Democracy* (New York, 1961), chap. xvix.

sible a division of the House membership of each party into "interested" and relatively "indifferent" congressmen on each of the four sets of issues. Evidence of party pressures will be sought in the voting relationships of "interested" and "indifferent" members of each party.[15] In dealing with votes of the various blocs within the House, use will be made of two rather simple measuring devices suggested by Stuart A. Rice[16] and employed by Julius Turner[17] — the index of likeness and the index of cohesion. The likeness index gauges the similarity of outlook of two voting blocs. For a given motion, an index of likeness is calculated by subtracting from 100 the difference between the percentages of "aye" votes cast by two blocs. Thus, if blocs of Republican "farm" and "nonfarm" congressmen both unanimously support a motion, their index of likeness is 100. If each bloc unanimously opposes the other, their index of likeness is zero. If one bloc divides 90–10 and the other 70–30, their likeness index is 80. The index of cohesion measures the degree of unity exhibited by any voting bloc. A unanimous vote for or against a motion earns a group a cohesion index of 100. A 50–50 division — that is, an outcome that would result from a random casting of votes — receives a cohesion index of zero. An index of cohesion for a bloc on any motion is the absolute difference between the percentage of "aye" and the percentage of "nay" votes cast. Thus, if a

15. "Party pressure" is as hazy a concept as "constituency pressure." Turner defined "political pressure" as "a force which brings about distinctive voting behavior on the part of Congressmen, whether the force is applied through conventional types of coercion or through the appeals of loyalties and ideologies." Turner, *Party and Constituency*, p. 11. The same definition will be used here; information about "party pressure" in Congress will be sought not in a review of the strong-arm actions of party leaders, but by inference from quantitative data.

16. Stuart A. Rice, "The Behavior of Legislative Groups: A Method of Measurement," *Political Science Quarterly*, 40:60–72 (March 1925); Rice, *Quantitative Methods in Politics*.

17. Turner, *Party and Constituency*, pp. 26, 36–37.

group votes 80–20 or 20–80 on a motion, its index of cohesion is 60.

Likeness and cohesion indices are derived from gross voting figures for blocs; the records of individual congressmen are not reached. In each of the following chapters, however, more intensive examination will be given to the votes of congressmen from the four kinds of "interested" districts. Some congressmen stay in office long enough to compile elaborate voting records; others come and go very quickly, making analysis of their stands on particular issues difficult or impossible. This problem will be overcome (or at least circumvented) in the following fashion: attention will be given not to the records of individuals but to the combined records of all members of one party serving a given district during the sixteen-year period. If, for example, an "interested" district sent four different Democrats and four different Republicans to the eight Congresses, the roll call votes cast by the four Democrats will be treated as one district "voting record" and the votes of the Republicans as another. A cumulative "party loyalty score" will be calculated for each series of party members serving each "interested" district. A "party loyalty score" simply records the proportion of votes, of a set of votes, cast in accordance with the positions of party majorities.[18] Thus, if all postwar Republican congressmen from one farm district voted with House Republican majorities on forty of fifty postwar farm roll calls, they will be assigned a combined party loyalty score, on farm issues, of 80.

The sources relied upon in this study are exclusively public sources — House roll call votes and House floor debates. All

18. In calculating party loyalty records, Turner used data only for roll calls on which party majorities opposed each other. Turner, *Party and Constituency*, pp. 78–79. No such restriction is enforced here; roll calls are included in the calculations regardless of the relative positions of the parties in voting on them.

roll call data are taken from the *Congressional Quarterly Almanac*. (It should be added that the positions of congressmen expressed in special "pairs" on specific roll calls are included in the following chapters as roll call "votes.") Whatever goes on in the anterooms of the Capitol, the spotlight here will be on the public faces of congressmen — the faces they choose to present to their electorates.

2/THE PARTIES AND THE FARMER

"I would like to make a few general observations about this bill and about agriculture. In the race to reach outer space, the planets, and to get out of this world, some people seem to forget that the most basic factor in our national existence on earth is agriculture. We should never forget the moral of the legend of the semigod, Hercules, wrestling with the giant, Antaeus, that the further away from the land we go the weaker we become, and the closer to the soil we stay the stronger we get."
— CONGRESSMAN ALFRED E. SANTANGELO
OF MANHATTAN[1]

NO SUBJECT OF POLITICAL CONCERN permits a clearer identification of constituency interest than agriculture. Congressmen from the shrinking array of districts dominated by farmers need little insight to detect what issue most easily roils their constituents. Especially since the 1920's, when evidence of the impact of the market economy upon agriculture became inescapable, farmers have sought political relief for their economic ills. No recent Congress has finally "solved" the agricultural problem, but none has been able to avoid dealing with it.

Farmers have been and are impelled to political action by a basic instability of income. Those who depend upon market sales suffer from a lack of control over their collective volume of production. With costs fairly constant, demand for farm goods relatively inelastic, and production regulated only by free competition, farmers are at the mercy of fluctuating com-

1. *Congressional Record,* June 6, 1961, p. 9592.

modity prices. Since 1929, the more comprehensive government agricultural programs have sought to bring production of major farm commodities into line with demand and thus to stabilize farm income. These programs, however, have typically turned out to be — under various euphemisms — subsidy programs. A program exchanging price supports for acreage restrictions quickly becomes a subsidy program when scientific cultivation produces commodity surpluses on the reduced acreage. The farmers, though most interested in commodity prices, have been given federal aid in other areas since 1933. To cite two examples, the rural electrification and soil conservation programs are of long duration and of sporadic political concern.

One central feature which characterizes farm programs — whether major or peripheral — is that they almost invariably cost the taxpayers or the consumers money. Hence, congressional reaction to agricultural pressures should be roughly predictable. It is equally to be expected that congressmen from farm areas should champion farm programs and that nonfarm congressmen should greet them without enthusiasm.

The evidence presented in Figure 1 suggests that this was indeed the case in the McNary-Haugen controversy of the 1920's. The long and finally unsuccessful campaign to enact the McNary-Haugen proposals was the first effort by the major farm organizations to put across a federal price support program; the modern era in agricultural politics began, in effect, in the middle 1920's. Neither political party, confronted by something unprecedented, knew quite what to do. Figure 1 demonstrates that congressmen simply voted according to their district interests. Midwestern and Western congressmen of both parties supported the new program from the start. Spokesmen for Southern cotton were at first unimpressed by the complex "equalization fee" and tariff arrangements of the

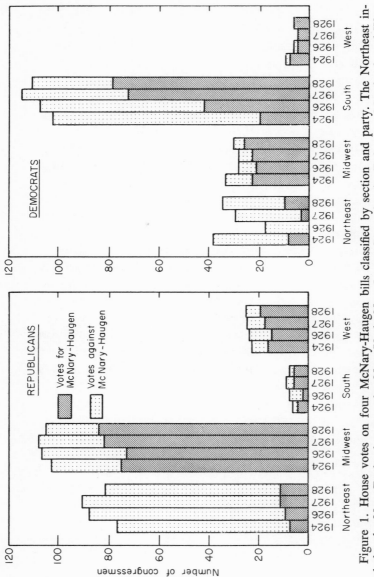

Figure 1. House votes on four McNary-Haugen bills classified by section and party. The Northeast includes the New England states, plus New York, New Jersey, Pennsylvania, Delaware, Maryland, and West Virginia. The Midwest includes Ohio, Indiana, Illinois, Michigan, Wisconsin, Minnesota, Iowa, Missouri, North Dakota, South Dakota, Nebraska, and Kansas. The South includes the Confederacy, plus Kentucky and Oklahoma. The West includes the eleven Mountain and Pacific states.

McNary-Haugen plan, but a drop in cotton prices and an invitation to cotton growers to write their own commodity proposals facilitated a historic "marriage of corn and cotton." [2] The conversion of Southern cotton, tobacco, and rice congressmen produced the House margin of victory for McNary-Haugen in 1927 and 1928. At no time, however, did Democrats or Republicans from the urban Northeast display much sympathy for the new departure. (Their lack of fervor was shared by President Coolidge, who vetoed each bill put before him.)

The breakdown by section in Figure 1 provides only a rough constituency index, but a closer examination would reveal that the division between farm and nonfarm congressmen was almost perfect. Most Midwestern city Republicans, for instance, opposed the program.[3] Despite Coolidge's laissez-faire expostulations, and despite reports that the Tammany delegation would support the McNary-Haugen plan in order to embarrass the President, the effect of party in the House voting was nearly nonexistent. Farm congressmen, assisted by a congressional failure to reapportion seats after the 1920 Census, had the votes in the House to pass their program themselves and, after achieving unity, proceeded to do so. H. L. Mencken's explanation of farm politics was short and direct: "The farmers, of course, we have with us always. They are chronic and incurable mendicants." [4]

2. See Gilbert C. Fite, *George N. Peek and the Fight for Farm Parity* (Norman, Okla., 1954), chap. x.

3. For a congressional district map showing positions of individual congressmen on the 1927 McNary-Haugen bill, see John D. Black, "The McNary-Haugen Movement," *American Economic Review,* 18:426 (September 1928). The map gives no party breakdown.

4. *H. L. Mencken on Politics: A Carnival of Buncombe,* ed. Malcolm Moos (New York, 1960), p. 282.

FARM ISSUES AND FARM DISTRICTS

By 1946 the division in Congress on agricultural questions was no longer a division between farm and nonfarm Representatives. (Indeed, had it been so, the agricultural programs could not have been sustained in the postwar years; the Census Bureau had divested rural areas of their congressional majority.) The New Deal era, with its wholesale extermination of little pigs, its controversies surrounding Wallace and Tugwell, its persistent suggestion that farmers unenrolled in the Farm Bureau should be recipients of federal largess, had left as a legacy an abiding ideological cleavage between the two parties on agricultural matters.

What form did this partisanship take in Congress? How, in particular, did each of the two congressional parties contrive to deal with its farm element in the 1947–1962 period? Both Democrats and Republicans had to face the problem, for the possession by each party of a goodly number of safe farm constituencies is a constant in American politics of a hundred years' standing. The presumption here is that some clue to party operations can be detected in the relations that prevailed between farm and nonfarm members of each party in voting on farm issues. Both parties were divided between those forced to be very interested in the plight of the farmer and those who could afford to be relatively indifferent; the influence of party can perhaps be spotted most clearly in the votes of the "indifferents." (There was, of course, no *absolute* indifference on farm issues; city congressmen have been known to lament the price of bread.)

The methodology used here requires the setting aside of a block of congressional districts as "farm districts" and the definition of a number of postwar House roll call votes as "farm votes." The criteria for inclusion of both districts and votes are arbitrary. In the case of the districts, 1950 census figures have been used to construct an index showing the concentration of farmers in each congressional district. For each district, the percentage of persons in the total 1950 population who were involved in farm work in 1950 — including farm operators, members of their families, and hired laborers — has been determined.[5] Multiple sets of district figures, all based on 1950 population statistics, were required for states that revised their district boundaries once or more in the 1947–1962 period. Finally, each congressional district with 10 percent or more of its total 1950 population involved in farm work has been called a "farm district," and, therefore, any congressman from such a district a "farm congressman." In the Eightieth Congress there were 122 "farm congressmen"; after the 1950 reapportionment only 111.

Figure 2 shows the post-1952 farm districts (that is, the set of districts created by November, 1952, in accord with the dictates of the 1950 Census). Above the 10 percent cut-off line fall the bulk of districts in the old cotton and tobacco areas of the South, most of the districts in the dairy, wheat, and corn areas of the Midwest, and a scattering of ranching and irrigated farm districts in the plains and West. This index ranks districts according to farm population; a ranking according to total farm income would produce a map somewhat different from that in Figure 2. In particular, there would be more "farm districts" in the semiurbanized but agriculturally

5. The Census Bureau counted the "number of persons doing farm work or chores on the place during the calendar week preceding the enumeration," and included (1) farm operators who worked at least one hour a week, (2) members of operators' families who worked fifteen hours or more, (3) hired persons who did any work at all. A farm was defined (with some additions and qualifications) as a place of three acres or more, on which the value of agricultural products in 1949 exceeded $150. Data on farmers were taken from U.S. Bureau of the Census, *U.S. Census of Agriculture: 1950,* I, Counties and State Economic Areas.

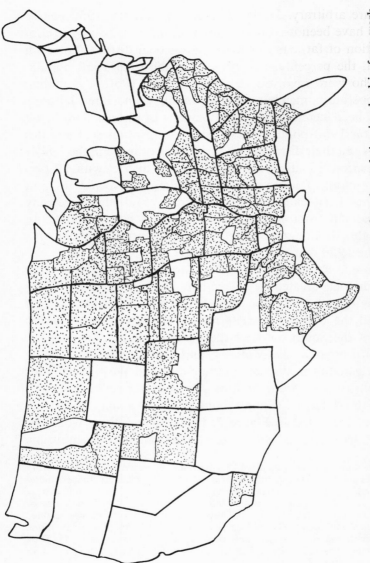

Figure 2. Congressional districts with 10 percent or more of total population involved in farm work. Occupational percentages are based on 1950 census figures; districts are those drawn after the 1950 reapportionment.

rich areas of Illinois, Indiana, and California. The population index has been chosen on the assumption that congressmen must finally be answerable to farmers as voters.

The next requirement for the analysis is a number of congressional roll call votes on issues that can be called farm issues. One hundred ten such votes have been selected from the voting records of the 1947–1962 period. Often there were several votes on the same piece of legislation, but on no two roll calls were the voting alignments exactly the same. The one essential feature which unites these 110 votes is that they were on issues of great concern to at least some farmers; in addition, they were typically not of transcendent concern to non-farmers.

Here the unity ceases. Adding together these votes is rather literally like adding apples and oranges; one of the roll calls, in fact, dealt with oranges. Some of the votes, such as the 1949 defeat of the Brannan Plan, were important; others were not. Some fifty-two votes dealt with omnibus price support programs or with programs for specific commodities. There were seven votes on the fortunes of oleo and ten votes on farm labor questions. Some twenty-six votes were on Department of Agriculture appropriations bills, and four dealt with reorganization of that department. Nine votes (including six of the appropriations votes and two of the reorganization votes) dealt with the Rural Electrification Administration.[6] Moreover, votes on commodity programs at the beginning and end of the sixteen-year period are not strictly comparable, for federal approaches to agriculture underwent some evolution in these years. Each

6. Of the remaining roll calls, three (1949, 1950, and 1954) were on the operations of the Commodity Credit Corporation, three (1951 and 1958) on the providing of marketing facilities for perishables, one (1957) on promotion of meat consumption, one (1959) on artificial coloring of oranges, four (1951) on proposed amendments — specifically affecting farm prices — to the Korean War Defense Production Act.

Secretary of Agriculture managed, at the least, to put a new gloss on basic farm policy.

One obvious problem which arises here, if it is to be assumed that the farm issues dealt with in these 110 votes were of concern to the previously defined "farm congressmen," is that several of the issues were clearly not of concern to all these congressmen. A Georgia legislator was not vitally interested in butter, a Nebraskan in tobacco, nor an Iowan in rice. In addition, the interests of spokesmen for different commodities obviously may conflict.[7] In the ascribing of a general "farm" content to these issues, a constituency interest has been attributed where it sometimes did not exist. One saving factor is that a good majority of these roll calls were on legislation affecting most or all farmers. A second saving factor is that there existed in these years, in fact, a community of interest among farm congressmen that cut across commodity bloc lines. When these blocs were not at odds — as they were in the oleo controversy of the 1940's and as they increasingly were on basic policy in the later years — congressional speakers for the major commodities tended to aid each other when specific commodity programs were at stake. Where this alliance was operative, it can be said that there existed a generalized and national farm constituency.

The above qualifications having been expressed, there remain 110 roll call votes on issues of more or less concern to a number of arbitrarily defined "farm congressmen." If the issues varied in content and changed over time, there still existed a continuous situation in which farm congressmen presumably represented their constituents in dealing with subjects of constituency concern. In each of the postwar Con-

7. An unsigned note entitled "The Political Impasse in Farm Support Legislation," *Yale Law Journal*, 71:952–978 (April 1962), provides an account of the various kinds of conflicts that arise between farmers growing different crops or growing the same crops under different conditions.

gresses there were between 9 and 23 votes on farm issues, and in the following analysis the votes from each Congress will frequently be treated, for purposes of demonstration, as a discrete set.

The assertion has been made that agricultural politics after the war was no longer nonpartisan, that congressmen no longer voted in the McNary-Haugen pattern simply as farmers or nonfarmers on farm issues. The point can be substantiated by citing cohesion indices for all farm and all nonfarm congressmen, party disregarded, on postwar farm roll calls. Average cohesion indices for each of the eight sessions of Congress are presented in Table 1. Two conclusions emerge from the

TABLE 1. Mean cohesion of farm and nonfarm congressmen on farm roll calls in postwar Congresses

	Congressional sessions							
	1947– 1948	1949– 1950	1951– 1952	1953– 1954	1955– 1956	1957– 1958	1959– 1960	1961– 1962
All farm	43	59	54	60	60	42	68	52
All nonfarm	28	29	12	31	20	23	25	28
Number of roll call votes	(16)	(13)	(11)	(9)	(12)	(13)	(13)	(23)

data. First, farm congressmen were considerably more united than their nonfarm brethren. The magnitude of the farm cohesion indices can be accounted for in part — but, as will be shown, only in part — by the fact that a considerable majority of "farm congressmen" were Southern Democrats with similar constituency interests. Second, cohesion among "indifferent" congressmen was exceedingly low. (It may be thought that nonfarm cohesion would be higher if "farm districts" were defined more liberally to include semirural areas. This is unlikely.) To cite some examples of voting by "indifferent" congressmen, on three of the most important postwar roll calls nonfarm congressmen divided almost evenly: on the 1949 motion defeating the Brannan Plan, 163–141; on the passage of the controversial price support bill opposed by the Eisenhower Administration in 1956, 149–172; and on the approval of President Kennedy's omnibus farm program in 1961, 145–172. The line of cleavage in Congress was clearly not between farmers and nonfarmers; a better hypothesis would be that farm members made use of divisions among their city cousins to accomplish their ends.

PARTY PRESSURES

The fact that nonfarm congressmen did not find it possible to unite on these postwar questions can be attributed incontestably to the influence of party. In Table 2, average cohesion indices for each of the eight Congressional sessions

TABLE 2. Mean cohesion of nonfarm congressmen by party on farm roll calls in postwar Congresses

	Congressional sessions							
	1947– 1948	1949– 1950	1951– 1952	1953– 1954	1955– 1956	1957– 1958	1959– 1960	1961 1962
Republican nonfarm	75	47	53	69	75	60	79	63
Democratic nonfarm	84	66	57	48	68	46	53	65
Mean cohesion of total nonfarm	28	29	12	31	20	23	25	28
Number of roll call votes	(16)	(13)	(11)	(9)	(12)	(13)	(13)	(23)

are given for nonfarm Democrats and nonfarm Republicans as well as for all nonfarm congressmen. A relatively high level of harmony did prevail within both party wings on agricultural votes. The suggestion is that the tug of party allegiance was far more influential among nonfarm congressmen than any general antipathy to farmers and their costly works.

This consistent maintenance, by both parties, of an impressive degree of cohesion among farm "indifferents" could hardly have been a purposeless exercise. What are the possibilities? Since the concern here is with the relationship in each party between farm and nonfarm congressmen, the principal question to be asked is: what bearing did the marshaling of party strength have on the fortunes of a party's farm members? Two patterns come immediately to mind. A party may embrace the programs put forth by its farm congressmen and seek acceptance of them among its members from more urban areas. Or a party may espouse policies more popular in the city than on the farm and try to sell them to its farm congressmen. In other words, party pressures may flow in opposite directions — either bolstering or undermining positions of farm members. The possibility that there existed such a directional difference in the legislative efforts of Democrats and Republicans will be tested in the following analysis. Some light can be thrown on the problem by examining the relative cohesion indices of farm and nonfarm wings of both parties and the voting records of party leaders on farm issues.

It may plausibly be assumed that a bloc of congressmen subjected to coinciding party and constituency pressures will demonstrate greater unity than a bloc subjected to conflicting pressures from party and constituency. (The assumption, of course, does not always hold. If constituency pressures are strong enough a group of congressmen will unite in defiance of party policy. Southern Democratic congressmen, for example, used to maintain unity on racial questions. In fact, opposing party and constituency pressures may be expected to produce low cohesion only when a congressional bloc views neither pressure as clearly and overwhelmingly more important than the other.) If the assumption is accepted as generally true, cohesion indices for party groupings can supply evidence of party pressure. In Figure 3, frequency distributions of cohesion indices, on the 110 postwar farm votes, are presented for farm and nonfarm segments of each party. The distributions for Democratic and Republican nonfarm congressmen look much alike. There emerges a striking difference, however, between the cohesion figures for the Democratic and Republican farm blocs. On more than half the roll calls, cohesion indices of farm Democrats are 90 or higher. On more than half the votes, indices of farm Republicans are below 60. Democratic farm congressmen were normally united in these years, Republican farm congressmen normally divided. The data point to a conclusion that the Democrats ordinarily threw the weight of party behind their farmers and that the Republicans put forth farm policies which provoked disunity in their farm wing.

A further clue may be gained from the cohesion figures by observing what effect partisan control of Congress or the Presidency had upon party unity in the House. In Table 3, cohesion figures for the 110 roll calls have been divided between those derived from votes under Democratic and under Republican Presidents. On the Republican side, a further subdivision has been made between votes in the five congressional sessions in which the party controlled the House or the Presidency, and those three in which it controlled neither. (No such Democratic division would be of use, for

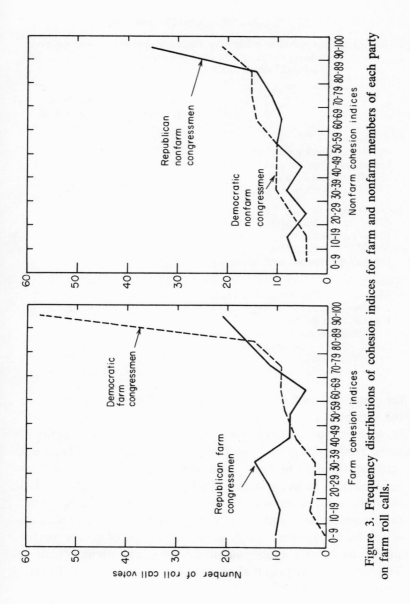

Figure 3. Frequency distributions of cohesion indices for farm and nonfarm members of each party on farm roll calls.

TABLE 3. Mean cohesion indices for farm and nonfarm congressmen of each party on farm roll calls with different parties in control of the Presidency and Congress, 1947–1962

	Farm congressmen	Nonfarm congressmen
Democrats		
63 roll call votes under		
Presidents Truman and Kennedy	79	68
47 roll call votes under		
President Eisenhower	82	54
Republicans		
47 roll call votes under		
President Eisenhower	49	71
63 roll call votes under		
Presidents Truman and Kennedy	58	61
Republicans		
63 roll call votes under President		
Eisenhower and in the Republican		
Eightieth Congress	49	72
47 roll call votes in three Demo-		
cratic Congresses under Demo-		
cratic Presidents	62	56

the party was out of power completely for only two years in the sixteen.)

With all due allowance made for the fact that variations in issues render dangerous any comparison of figures for different sessions, the data in Table 3 are highly suggestive. The figures indicate that the incumbency of a Democratic President tended to unite a bit more effectively the Democratic "indifferent" congressmen, and without impinging upon the high cohesion of the party's farmers. Republican possession of power tended simply to unite Republican nonfarmers and divide farmers. The previous conclusion about the flow of pressures within the parties is reinforced.

The thrust of the argument is clear. A final nail can be driven into place with an inspection of the House voting records of elected party leaders. (The position of party leadership is taken to be discernible in the votes of the two top officials voting in each party — the Majority Leader and Majority Whip or Minority Leader and Minority Whip — , or in the vote of one of these officials if the position of the other is not recorded.) The underlying assumption here is that the votes of elected leaders on farm issues normally reflected the official positions of their parties. The leaders' votes can be used to demonstrate the manner in which farm congressmen were treated in each party. If a party is divided into Bloc A and Bloc B, its leaders may be assumed to be summoning party strength to back Bloc A rather than Bloc B if their recorded position on an issue is that of a significantly higher proportion of members of Bloc A than of Bloc B. Here the blocs in question are the farm and nonfarm wings of each party. Farm and nonfarm Republicans differed significantly on 78 of the 110 postwar farm votes, farm and nonfarm Democrats on 65. (The chi square test has been used here, with significance at the .05 level.) The records of Republican and Democratic leaders on these votes where their flocks were divided are strikingly different; the following figures indicate respectively the number of times the leaders of a party favored the farm position, the number of times they were divided themselves, and the number of times they favored the nonfarm position.

Republicans	19	12	47
Democrats	49	6	10

On votes where farm and nonfarm elements were in disagreement, Democratic leaders placed the weight of party behind their farmers more than 75 percent of the time. Republican leaders bolstered the position of their farmers less than 25 percent of the time.

The cohesion data and the leadership voting records all point to the same conclusion. Party pressures on agricultural issues did flow in opposite directions in these years. The impressive unity of farm Democrats and the sympathy displayed for their positions by party leaders indicate that it was the custom for the Democratic party to embrace programs favored by its farmers. The disunity of farm Republicans and the predilections of their party leaders indicate that the Republican party espoused farm policies less popular on the farm than off it.

PARTY AND COMMITTEE LEADERS

The analysis so far is statistical and skeletal; it will help at this point to add a little flesh to it. It will be necessary also to take notice of some exceptions to the general voting pattern — exceptions on some peripheral programs throughout the 1947–1962 period and on major commodity policies as the era drew to a close.

What are the centers of power in farm politics? Students of Congress naturally focus attention on the House Agriculture Committee — one of the most powerful of congressional committees, the stronghold of leading commodity interests, and the prime mover behind agricultural legislation in the house.[8] Votes on agriculture are almost always votes for or against programs offered by the Agriculture Committee, and a perusal

8. Two recent studies of the Committee are those of Charles O. Jones: "Representation in Congress: The Case of the House Agriculture Committee," *American Political Science Review*, 55:358–367 (June 1961), and "The Role of the Congressional Subcommittee," *Midwest Journal of Political Science*, 6:327–344 (November 1962).

of the records of recent decades would show that the committee, when reasonably united, has usually had its way.

What allowed the Committee to win its victories in the period in question, however — what indeed saved its program from decimation by the nonfarm majority in the House — was the partisan context within which it operated. The conflicting pressures of the two parties, when translated into votes, created a recurrent pattern of opposing coalitions on farm issues. It was the custom for a solid core of Democratic farm congressmen to unite with a good majority of nonfarm Democrats and a substantial number of farm Republicans in opposing an overwhelming majority of nonfarm Republicans. Six important farm roll calls exemplifying this voting pattern in its more exaggerated form are listed in Table 4. (On each vote the ayes are given first and the nays second. Thus the affirmative or negative direction of each vote reveals the attitude of a party wing toward a particular House motion, and not toward the farm population.)

The key to the success of the farm bloc lay, in short, in its ability to achieve a degree of bipartisan harmony among Republican and Democratic farm congressmen, and then to enlist the aid of the Democratic party and its leadership in supplying the margin of victory for its programs. Offensives thus proceeded on three fronts: appeals had to be made to farm Democrats, to farm Republicans, and to urban and industrial Democrats. Significant defections in any one of these three groups could endanger the farm bloc position. The floor tactics of this Democratic-centered farm coalition can be demonstrated by citing a rather typical incident that took place in 1951.[9] A Republican amendment cutting a substantial amount from the Commodity Credit Corporation

9. *Congressional Record,* April 9–19, 1951, pp. 3558–3587.

TABLE 4. Votes of farm and nonfarm congressmen of each party on six important farm roll calls, 1947–1962

		Votes			
			Dem.		Rep.
Year	Issue	Dem. farm cong'- men	non- farm cong'- men	Rep. farm cong'- men	non- farm cong'- men
1947	Vote to recede from House Conference position, to override Republican leadership and restore A.A.A. soil conservation funds	62–0	98–1	25–24	18–162
1952	Vote to extend 90% of parity program for basic commodities	57–0	90–44	33–2	42–89
1954	Substitution of Benson 82.5% of parity program for House Agriculture Committee's 90% program	2–69	44–87	19–19	172–5
1956	Passage of Administration-opposed high parity program	69–2	124–33	25–12	25–139
1958	Attempt to suspend the rules and pass Senate omnibus bill as amended by House Agriculture Committee	70–6	117–35	20–11	22–142
1961	Vote on President Kennedy's omnibus farm program (modified)	68–3	117–58	24–8	28–114

budget unexpectedly and narrowly won in the Committee of the Whole. The next day three congressmen — Jamie Whitten (D. Mississippi), Clifford Hope (R. Kansas), and Adolph Sabath (D. Illinois) — were summoned to explain to their colleagues the enormity of the action, and the vote was decisively overridden. The coalition was restored. Whitten was an important farm Democrat, Hope the leader of the Republican farm bloc, and Sabath the dean of Northern city Democrats.

The extent to which the Agriculture Committee, speaking for the farm bloc, achieved its aims by working within the orbit of the Democratic party can hardly be overstated. The figures given below suggest, on the one hand, the closeness of the relationship between Democratic Committee leaders and Democratic party leaders, and, on the other hand, the relative distance between the positions of Republican Committee leaders and their party hierarchy. The figures show respectively how often the elected leaders of each party agreed with their top Agriculture Committee member, were divided themselves, and disagreed with their top Committee member, on roll calls where farm and nonfarm blocs of the party were significantly divided (and where the relevant people recorded their positions).

Republicans	38	9	27
Democrats	50	4	6

Clifford Hope of Kansas, Chairman of or ranking Republican on the Committee until 1957, as often as not joined the Democrats in opposing the farm policies of his own party.

House Republican leaders, backed with some consistency after 1949 by the Farm Bureau, proclaimed as their goal in this postwar period the abandonment or curtailment of most of the major and minor farm programs sustained by the federal government. Their legislative strategy was dictated by the fact that the Republican leadership in the sixteen-year period never, not even in the Eightieth Congress, possessed effective control of the Agriculture Committee. In 1953–1954 the Committee was formally in Republican hands for a second time, but it refused to accept the farm program of Agriculture Secretary Ezra Taft Benson.

With a number of party farm congressmen trafficking with the Democrats, and with no committee as a base for operations, the Republican leadership had a difficult time in advancing its policies. In the Eightieth Congress the Republican leaders, in firm control of the Subcommittee on Agriculture of the House Appropriations Committee, tried to overhaul existent farm programs by drastically reducing — in some cases abolishing — appropriations for them. Their success was not complete, for they encountered the opposition of House Democrats, the Truman Administration, the Senate, the Farm Bureau, and Chairman Hope's Agriculture Committee. In 1954 the Republicans secured passage of the Benson farm program by substituting it on the floor for the Committee program; the Administration successfully tailored its policies to divide the Republican farm membership. After 1954, with the attenuation of farmer esteem for Secretary Benson, the Republicans fell back upon the veto power of the President to force through their basic programs. The use of the veto was rather successful, for the major commodity blocs often needed to have their programs renewed or revised; the Eisenhower programs were better than no new programs at all. On one issue of great concern to farmers, the proposed reorganization of the Rural Electrification Administration to take final authority over loans away from Secretary Benson, the Democratic-centered coalition came very close to overriding the President's veto, but failed.

Democratic Presidents usually chose to work through the House Agriculture Committee and not against it, thus reinforcing rather than undermining the power of the House farm bloc. The Truman Administration and the Committee were generally in accord on measures that reached the floor. The Kennedy Administration submitted its agricultural programs and then accepted alterations necessary to please the House

Committee. The one major program that a Democratic Administration tried to enact without the support of at least its own farm congressmen was the 1949 Brannan Plan. Even here the Truman Administration obtained a favorable Committee vote for a modified version of the plan, but substantial numbers of farm congressmen in both parties were opposed and the plan was therefore defeated on the floor. The voting indicates that on this occasion the Democratic party was atypically trying to override the farm bloc rather than acting as its agent. The immediate issue was a motion substituting the conventional 90 percent of parity program for the Truman proposals, a motion on which farm Democrats, nonfarm Democrats, farm Republicans, and nonfarm Republicans voted respectively as follows:

$$46\text{--}33 \qquad 35\text{--}139 \qquad 36\text{--}2 \qquad 128\text{--}2$$

There were other exceptions to the general pattern; the Democratic-centered coalitions ordinarily in evidence on major commodity legislation were not evoked on some other issues of the period. One way to distinguish among issues is to measure relative degrees of agreement within the parties on different issues. (The normal pattern ought to be one of agreement between farm and nonfarm Democrats, and relative disagreement between nonfarm Republicans and their straying farmers.) Likeness indices for the two blocs within each party on various types of issues are given in Table 5.

In the votes on rural electrification, on Department of Agriculture appropriations, and on the commodity programs, the Republicans tended to isolate their farm wing and the Democrats to rally behind theirs. The Democratic party was, in fact, the servant of a bipartisan farm bloc. The inclination of farm congressmen representing various commodity interests to vote for each other's programs is demonstrated in the note-

TABLE 5. Mean likeness indices for farm and nonfarm wings of each party on sets of roll calls dealing with different kinds of farm issues, 1947–1962

Subject area	No. of roll calls	Mean likeness indices for Dem. farm and nonfarm cong'men	Mean likeness indices for Rep. farm and nonfarm cong'men	Difference between Democratic and Republican indices
Oleo: votes on federal taxation of oleo, and its use by Navy	7	92	54	+ 38
Rural electrification: votes on appropriations, administrative organization, and initiation of rural telephone program	9	93	58	+ 35
Appropriations: votes on Department of Agriculture budget, 80th Congress	13	95	72	+ 23
Omnibus bills: votes on omnibus farm programs in 1949, 1952, 1954, 1955, 1956, 1958, 1961	17	80	60	+ 20
Corn, wheat, and feed grains: votes on programs in the 85th Congress dealing with corn, in the 86th dealing with wheat, in the 87th dealing with wheat and feed grains	16	89	74	+ 15
Southern commodities: votes on programs dealing specifically with cotton, tobacco, peanuts, and rice	10	79	64	+ 15
Defense production: votes on farm price amendments to the Korean War Defense Production Act in 1951	4	55	73	− 18
Farm labor: votes on child farm labor and the Mexican farm labor program	10	55	81	− 26

worthy fact that Republicans were less united than Democrats in voting on Southern as well as on Midwestern commodities. The oleo votes seem to fit the conventional pattern, but of course this is deceptive. That there were fallen Republican farmers (as defined for the moment by these likeness indices) does not necessarily imply that there was Democratic seduction. On oleo questions the Republican dairy congressmen stood alone and were flattened by a bipartisan alliance of spokesmen for consumers and spokesmen for Southern cotton growers eager to sell cottonseed oil to oleo producers. The bottom figures in Table 5 provide other exceptions to the general rule; in votes on Korean War Defense Production Act amendments affecting farm prices, and on farm labor questions, farm and nonfarm Democrats were farther apart than farm and nonfarm Republicans. The Mexican bracero program was the only farm program kept alive with Republican rather than Democratic assistance; liberal and labor groups opposed it, but few Republican congressmen had any qualms about a federal subsidy program the product of which was cheap labor.

It must be said also that House voting patterns varied over time as well as according to issue. The outline of farm politics presented here has been one suggesting considerable stability in coalition alignments — an outline of Democrats supporting year in and year out the programs of a bipartisan farm bloc, and of Republicans, deserted by their own farm wing, trying in vain to win House majorities. In fact, the treatment of the sixteen-year period as a unit conceals secular trends not fully evident in the gross roll call figures. The modern farm bloc in the House — that is, the bipartisan alliance of commodity interests inhabiting the Agriculture Committee — had to endure after 1949 the antipathy of the Farm Bureau and in the middle 1950's began slowly to disintegrate. Stanley Andrews argues that the adoption of the Eisenhower farm program in

1954 "marked the beginning of the end of the Farm Bloc."[10]
The Eisenhower Administration successfully divided the Republican farm element and kept it divided. On most farm issues a number of Republican farm congressmen continued to vote with the Democrats, but a declining number deserted their party on major legislation. Twenty-four Republicans were recorded against the Benson program in 1954, but only four favored the undiluted version of President Kennedy's feed grains program in 1961. Finally, only one Republican could be rounded up to support the President's supply-management proposals for wheat and feed grains in 1962. A historic changeover occurred in 1959, with the accession of Charles Hoeven of Iowa to the top Republican position on the Agriculture Committee. Clifford Hope, a veteran of the agricultural struggles of earlier decades, had continued until the end of his career to work with the Democrats on farm policy. Hoeven, like Hope a critic of Republican farm programs in the 1940's and early 1950's, worked closely with Minority Leader Charles Halleck on farm matters during his tenure as committee leader.

Why did the farm bloc come apart? The divisive tactics of Benson's Agriculture Department doubtless had something to do with it, but there were deeper reasons having to do with changes in crop patterns. The power axis of the farm bloc was always an alliance of corn and cotton, and by the late 1950's that alliance had all but dissolved. Harmony among the different commodity blocs was possible as long as each bloc could write its own program and all the programs could be bound together with a plea for 90 percent of parity. What destroyed this harmony, more than anything else, was the rising problem of feed grains surpluses. Any solution to this

10. Stanley Andrews, *The Farmer's Dilemma* (Washington, D.C., 1961), p. 96.

problem affected not just corn growers in the Midwest but almost all farmers everywhere — not least of all the Southern farmers who had taken acreage out of tobacco and cotton and put it into livestock and feed grains. A program acceptable to all farmers was difficult to find, and the Democratic proposals for restriction of feed grains production predictably pleased congressmen from the South more than those from the Midwest. The result was a trend toward party-line voting on major agricultural programs. Republican congressmen in and out of the Corn Belt united in opposing the Kennedy feed grains program. Under Kennedy the Farm Bureau enjoyed stronger support from Corn Belt Republicans than it had received at any time since its desertion of 90 percent of parity in the late 1940's. Some of the freshman Republicans returned by Midwestern farm constituencies in 1960 — congressmen such as Ralph Beermann (Nebraska 3) and Paul Findley (Illinois 20) whose Republican predecessors had been party heretics on farm policy — actually joined House Republican leaders in decrying government involvement in agriculture.

The dissolution of the farm bloc entailed, of course, the destruction of the House Agriculture Committee as a cohesive political unit. Richard F. Fenno, Jr., in a study of the House Appropriations Committee, has portrayed Appropriations as an effectively "integrated" committee and argued that integration is facilitated by the existence of a firm consensus on committee goals or tasks.[11] The likelihood is that the Agriculture Committee was, in the immediate postwar years, similarly well "integrated." What better glue could there be than the pervasive notion that "something must be done" for each

11. Richard F. Fenno, Jr., "The House Appropriations Committee as a Political System: The Problem of Integration," *American Political Science Review*, 56:310–324 (June 1962).

commodity? The development by the commodity blocs of mutually exclusive goals, however, produced the committee of 1958 described by Charles O. Jones — a committee bifurcated along coinciding party and commodity lines, and one in which corn, wheat, and dairy Republicans were clearly accorded a place below the salt.[12] By the middle 1960's Congressman Richard Bolling could describe Agriculture as "the committee that is perhaps the most bitterly divided in a partisan sense." [13]

Despite the turn toward partisanship, however, the coalition patterns typical of earlier years had by no means disappeared in 1962. It is still fair to say that, throughout the sixteen-year period, Democratic agricultural policies found greater acceptance in the farm than in the nonfarm wing of the party, and that Republican policies stimulated defections from party ranks among farm rather than among nonfarm congressmen. A striking example of the treatment usually given by both parties to their farm members was provided in an incident that occurred during the Kennedy years.[14] New statutory restrictions on the planting of wheat provoked requests in 1961 from farmers in Kansas and surrounding areas for temporary authority to plant winter crops of feed grains. The congressmen who seemed to be most concerned were from the Fifth and Sixth districts in Kansas. There was an uncommon symmetry to their appeals, for one, J. Floyd Breeding, was a Democrat, and the other, Robert Dole, was a Republican. They asked for bipartisan support of their position and did in fact win support from the leaders of both parties. But the voting on their motion was not at all bipartisan; farm Democrats,

12. Jones, "The Role of the Congressional Subcommittee."
13. Richard Bolling, *House Out of Order* (New York, 1965), p. 96.
14. *Congressional Record,* September 18, 1961, pp. 20064–20069.

nonfarm Democrats, farm Republicans, and nonfarm Republicans voted respectively as follows:

68–2　　　　147–26　　　　13–17　　　　13–120

The Democrats came to the aid of their colleague and the Republicans did not. Since a two-thirds vote was required for a suspension of the rules, the bill was not passed. The coalition alignments on this vote are the alignments characteristic of postwar agricultural politics.

THE REPUBLICANS

An extemporaneous 1954 statement by Congressman Leon Gavin of Pennsylvania is a fair rendition of the postwar sentiments of rank-and-file Republican nonfarm congressmen on agriculture: "In the name of consumer sense stop this indefensible destruction of our liberties and follow the lead of President Eisenhower out of the wilderness of surpluses, waste, and disgusting dependence on the Government for a dole, and back to the common virtues of industry and thrift that made our State and Nation great." [15] For many Northeastern Republicans serving in these years, a distaste for price support programs was reinforced by the possession of a number of poultry and dairy farmer constituents interested in purchasing cheap feed grains.

The position of the Republican party and its leaders on farm matters was usually one reflecting the views of congressmen like Gavin, and hence not one that could be accepted with equanimity by congressmen subject to the wrath of Midwestern farmers. There is little doubt that the vigorous farm program of Secretary Benson, the only Republican Secretary

15. *Congressional Record,* June 30, 1954, p. 9365.

of Agriculture since President Hoover's Arthur M. Hyde, was instrumental in displacing a number of Midwestern Republican congressmen from office. (Benson's policies were widely thought to be political poison. One freshman Democrat elected in 1958 had these words: "I would not have beaten my opponent had he not been forced to go down the line with Republican policy. After the President vetoed the farm bill, he shifted position and voted against the bill. It was party pressure that did it.")[16]

The common result of conflicting party and constituency pressures was a fragmentation of the Republican farm wing in House voting. The fragmentation, however, was not random. The data presented in Figure 4 yield an impressive inverse correlation (minus .678) between the relative size of farm population in a district and the loyalty of the district's Republican congressmen to their party on farm issues.[17] Over the sixteen-year period, the more farmers a Republican congressman represented the more disposed he was to desert his party on farm votes. Heresy flourished in the heavily agricultural districts of the Corn Belt as well as in the poorer dairy districts and in the wheat areas of the plains.

The waywardness of some districts in Figure 4 merits comment. The deviant behavior — the rather high party loyalty scores — of Republicans from the Third Nebraska district can probably be attributed to the fact that the district's

16. Quoted in Clapp, *The Congressman*, p. 319.
17. In the calculation of party loyalty scores for Figure 4 and for succeeding figures and tables, scores have been determined not for each congressman but for each district. A district score is based on the votes on all farm issues of all congressmen from one party serving the district in the postwar period. A district is included in the totals for a party if it elected members of the party to at least three Congresses, and if these congressmen voted on at least ten farm roll calls. Districts are taken to be continuous units throughout the sixteen-year period if their boundaries went unchanged, if they suffered only minor boundary changes, or if incumbent congressmen survived boundary changes.

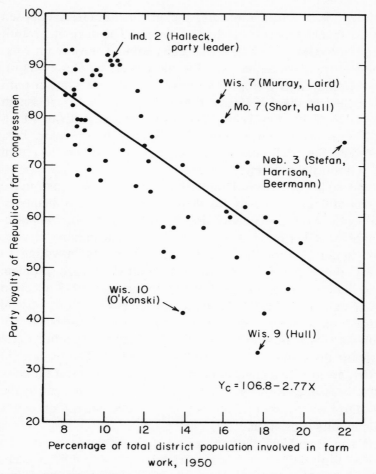

Figure 4. Relation between size of district farm population and loyalty of Republican farm congressmen on farm issues. Data are included here for 26 marginal farm districts with between 8.0 and 9.9 percent of total population involved in farm work.

farmers were cattle ranchers; the grazing interests opposed government support of feed grains prices. The deviant Seventh Wisconsin district lay in a rich dairy area. The Seventh Missouri district was represented for many years by Dewey Short, who displayed in Congress an unvarnished conservatism until his defeat in the 1956 farm revolt. Republican Congressmen from the Ninth and Tenth Wisconsin districts, both of which appear some distance below the Figure 4 regression line, reflected the traditional Progressive outlook of northwestern Wisconsin dairy farmers.

On some occasions House Republican leaders did make direct attempts to satisfy the demands of their farm members. In 1949, Minority Leader Joe Martin voted with the farm minority of his party in favor of the rural telephone service, and again in 1950 he joined a farm minority in voting to solve the Commodity Credit Corporation storage problem that had received so much publicity in the 1948 election campaign. In 1953, the Republican leaders worked for special legislation to rescue some Maryland tobacco farmers, in Republican districts, who had previously voted not to join federal support programs and then come to regret it. The leaders, in 1961, voted with a party minority to aid Kansas wheat farmers. But these occasions on which party leaders went against the nonfarm wing were rare and did not include activity on major commodity legislation.

Farm Republicans often voiced their displeasure with the party. With dairy congressmen traditionally Republican, Representative Harold Knutson of Minnesota could not accept the attitude of the Eightieth Congress toward oleo: "New Deal Congresses had 16 years in which to take up oleo tax repeal, but it was too hot for them, so a group of Republicans obligingly does it for them . . . I wish I had time to pay my compliments to the Republicans who signed the discharge rule in the way I really should like." [18] Usher Burdick, a choleric representative of North Dakota wheat farmers, was outspoken in criticism of his party and its leaders. On the Brannan Plan: "Will history never make a dent on the minds of the Republican Party?" [19] On the 1958 freeze of price supports: "I hate to see the Democratic Party the only party in this Congress that can see any protection for farmers . . . Secretary Benson has done damage enough without having a bunch of Representatives tagging along supporting him." [20] The difficulties of farm members were often painfully clear. In the Eightieth Congress a number of first-term Republicans from Missouri, where rural electrification had been very popular, were forced to decide whether to oppose the party in its efforts to slash R. E. A. funds. Most of the congressmen supported the party position in 1947, but could no longer do so in 1948; they were no longer in Congress in 1949. In 1956 Congressman Henry Dixon, representing Utah ranchers, delivered a speech covering a full page in the *Congressional Record* in support of an amendment to include grazing lands in the soil bank program. Then, after party leader Halleck had examined the amendment, Dixon proceeded to vote against it.[21] The course of many farm congressmen, such as Clifford Hope, was to refrain from criticizing the party leadership but to depend upon Democratic votes to protect their districts.

The record on roll calls during the sixteen postwar years was one of persistent defection from party ranks by Republican farm congressmen on farm issues. Figure 5 provides a frequency distribution of party loyalty scores, on farm votes, for Republican congressmen from all farm districts served by Republicans in at least three of the eight postwar Congresses.

18. *Congressional Record,* April 26, 1948, p. 4858.
19. *Congressional Record,* July 20, 1949, p. 9853.
20. *Congressional Record,* March 20, 1958, p. 4901.
21. *Congressional Record,* May 3, 1956, pp. 7423–7424, 7447.

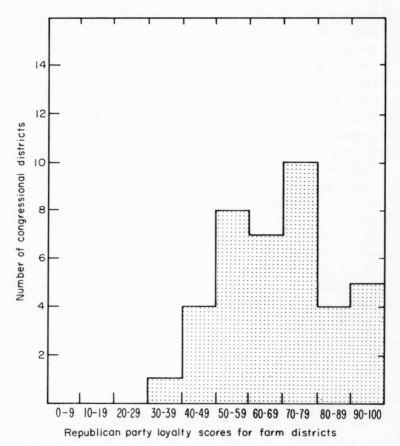

Figure 5. Frequency distribution of party loyalty scores for Republican farm districts.

The twenty-five districts whose congressmen ranked lowest in loyalty scores are given in Table 6, along with the congressmen and the scores. In the immediate postwar years the Ninth Wisconsin and Ninth Minnesota districts, first and fourth

TABLE 6. Farm districts whose Republican congressmen ranked lowest in party loyalty on farm issues, 1947–1962

District	Congressmen	No. of recorded votes of all district cong'men	Percent of total population in each district involved in farming	Party loyalty score for all congressmen serving each district
Wis. 9	Hull	42	17.7	33
Wis. 10	O'Konski	99	13.9	41
N.D. AL	Robertson, Burdick, Nygaard	88	18.0	41
Minn. 9	Hagen, Langen	81	19.2	46
S.D. 1	Mundt, Lovre, Reifel	79	18.2	49
Ia. 3	Gwynne, Gross	101	13.4	52
Ia. 6	Dolliver	56	16.6	52
Kans. 5	Hope	59	12.9	53
Minn. 7	Andersen	105	19.8	55
Ia. 2	Talle, Bromwell	91	12.9	58
Ia. 8	Hoeven	104	13.4	58
S.D. 2	Case, Berry	106	14.9	58
Kans. 6	Smith, Dole	107	18.5	59
Ia. 4	LeCompte, Kyl	97	16.2	60
Neb. 1	Curtis, Weaver	98	14.2	60
N.D. AL	Lemke, Aandahl, Krueger, Short	94	18.0	60
Wis. 3	Stevenson, Withrow, Thomson	102	16.1	61
Ia. 7	Jensen	104	17.0	62
Kans. 1	Cole, Avery	99	12.3	65
Ill. 20	Simpson, Mrs. Simpson, Findley	108	11.5	66
Minn. 1	Andresen, Quie	105	13.9	70
Minn. 2	O'Hara, Nelsen	98	16.7	70
Colo. 2	Hill, Dominick	91	10.0	71
Mont. 2	D'Ewart, Fjare, Battin	79	12.1	71
Neb. 4	Miller, Martin	94	17.1	71

on the list, returned Republican Representatives — Merlin Hull and Harold C. Hagen — who had served respectively as Progressive and Farmer-Labor congressmen in previous years. Among those who represented dissenting districts listed in Table 6 are all four men who rose to the top party position on the Agriculture Committee in the postwar decades; their *personal* loyalty scores were: Clifford Hope, 53; August Andresen, 67; William Hill, 67; and Charles Hoeven, 58. And prominent on the list — all with cumulative party loyalty scores well below 70 — are the six heavily agricultural districts in the rich and Republican Iowa Corn Belt.

THE DEMOCRATS

The statement has been made that the House farm bloc achieved its postwar legislative successes because of the aid it received from the Democratic party. That is to say, the positions of Democratic and many Republican farm congressmen were accepted and supported by Democrats from urban and industrial areas. Some evidence for this argument is offered in Figure 6, a frequency distribution of likeness indices for farm and nonfarm Democrats and for farm and nonfarm Republicans on the 110 postwar roll calls. The data indicate that the Democrats were able to preserve an extraordinary unity on farm matters and that their harmony contrasted sharply with Republican disharmony. It was noted earlier that cohesion figures for nonfarm Democrats and nonfarm Republicans are quite comparable; the explanation for this similarity lies in the striking fact that the Democrats were about as successful in marshaling support for farm programs among their nonfarm congressmen as the Republicans were in marshaling opposition among theirs.

Why Democrats from urban or semiurban areas should

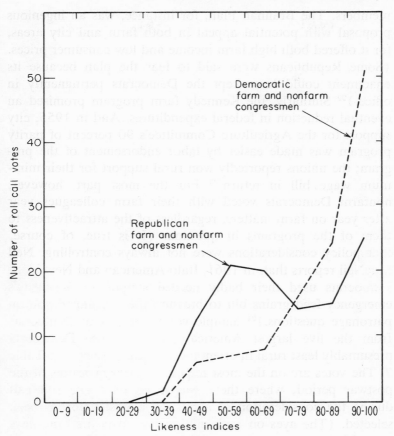

Figure 6. Frequency distributions of likeness indices for farm and nonfarm Republicans and for farm and nonfarm Democrats on 110 postwar farm roll calls.

have displayed solicitude for the farmer is not at all clear, especially since the programs of the Agriculture Committee were often costly. At times the Democratic party did make a conscious effort to put forth programs attractive to its city members. The Brannan Plan, for instance, was an ingenious proposal with potential appeal in both farm and city areas, for it offered both high farm income and low consumer prices. (Some Republicans were said to fear the plan because its enactment could have kept the Democrats permanently in office.)[22] Similarly, the Kennedy farm program promised an eventual reduction in federal expenditures. And in 1955, city support for the Agriculture Committee's 90 percent of parity program was made easier by labor endorsement of the program; the unions reportedly won rural support for their minimum wage bill in return.[23] For the most part, however, nonfarm Democrats voted with their farm colleagues year after year on farm matters, regardless of the attractiveness to them of the programs in question. (It is true, of course, that policy considerations were not always controlling. Neil MacNeil reports that, in 1961, Italo-American and New York Democrats used their badly needed support of Kennedy's emergency feed grains bill to pressure the Administration on patronage questions.)[24] Sample voting records of Democrats from the five largest American cities — those Democrats presumably least rural in orientation — are presented in Table 7. The votes are on the most important farm measures of the postwar period; where there was more than one roll call during the consideration of a bill the closest vote has been selected. (The ayes on each motion are given first, the nays second.)

The record in Table 7 is, in general, one of agreement

22. See Reo M. Christenson, *The Brannan Plan: Farm Politics and Policy* (Ann Arbor, 1959), p. 143.

23. See J. Roland Pennock, "Party and Constituency in Postwar Agricultural Price-Support Legislation," *Journal of Politics*, 18:167–210 (May 1956).

24. Neil MacNeil, *Forge of Democracy: The House of Representatives* (New York, 1963), pp. 249–251.

TABLE 7. Votes of Democratic congressmen from the five largest American cities on fourteen important postwar farm roll calls

Year	Issue	New York	Philadelphia	Detroit	Chicago	Los Angeles	Total from five cities	Total farm Dems
1949	Defeat of modified Brannan Plan by substitution of conventional 90% of parity program	0–16	0–4	0–4	0–10	0–4	0–38	46–33
1952	Extension of 90% of parity program	0–18	0–4	4–0	2–2	3–1	10–25	57–0
1954	Substitution of Benson program for Agriculture Committee's 90% program	5–8	4–1	2–2	1–5	0–4	12–20	2–69
1955	Passage of Agriculture Committee's 90% program	12–4	5–0	6–0	8–1	4–0	35–5	71–2
1956	Passage of Agriculture Committee's 90% program	12–4	5–0	6–0	8–1	4–0	35–5	69–2
1957	Attempted passage of Republican corn program	0–16	0–5	0–6	0–8	0–4	0–39	30–49
1958	Attempted recommittal of Democratic resolution freezing farm support prices	3–13	0–3	0–6	2–6	0–4	5–32	1–74
1958	Attempt to bring to floor Agriculture Committee's omnibus farm program	7–9	0–5	6–0	6–2	1–3	20–19	77–0
1958	Attempt to suspend the rules and pass Senate omnibus bill as amended by House Agriculture Committee	11–5	5–0	6–0	7–1	3–1	32–7	70–6
1959	Vote on conference report of wheat bill agreed upon by House Agriculture Committee	9–7	0–6	5–1	5–5	5–0	24–19	81–6
1960	Attempted recommittal of Agriculture Committee's wheat bill	6–9	6–0	0–6	1–8	0–5	13–28	12–71
1961	Passage of Kennedy feed grains program	17–1	6–0	6–0	10–0	5–0	44–1	61–15
1961	Passage of Kennedy omnibus farm program	15–2	1–5	5–1	8–2	4–1	33–11	68–3
1962	Recommittal vote on Kennedy omnibus program	1–17	0–6	0–6	0–10	0–5	1–44	18–61

between city and country. There are exceptions, one of which — the voting on the Brannan Plan — has been explained. In addition, city Democrats did not support the extension of the 90 percent of parity program in 1952, but it should be pointed out that their votes were not needed. The Republicans, doubtless because of the Korean War, temporarily dropped their objections to high farm subsidies and the extension was easily approved. The most serious city defections came in the late 1950's on some of the more expensive commodity programs — especially those involving wheat. The city-farm alliance was notably strong in the middle 1950's and after the Democratic recapture of the Presidency in 1960. J. R. Pennock presents persuasive evidence that the intervention of labor made the difference between defeat of the Agriculture Committee's program in 1954 and victory in 1955.[25] What may be as important, however, is that labor influence reinforced already existent predilections; Table 7 indicates that most city Democrats, at least from these five cities, were disposed to favor 90 percent of parity in 1954.

The voting figures indicate, unsurprisingly, that Democrats from a city often voted as a bloc. The Detroit congressmen, for instance, were united and extraordinarily loyal to party farm policies throughout the period, whereas the Philadelphia members often deserted the party. The Chicago congressmen, with the frequent exception of Sidney Yates, followed the party line. A fair conclusion might be that the party leadership was more successful in marshaling farm support among machine Democrats than among more independent members from Northern industrial areas. For example, Abraham Ribicoff, as a Hartford congressman, often voted against the party on farm matters; Otis Pike of Long Island could not be kept in line. Maryland and Rhode Island Democrats voted frequently with the Republicans. Among those especially loyal to the party were the senior Democrats from New York City; the city-farm alliance was given recognition in the 1950's in the appointment of Victor Anfuso of Brooklyn to the House Agriculture Committee and of Alfred Santangelo

25. Pennock, "Party and Constituency in Postwar Agricultural Price-Support Legislation."

of Manhattan to the Appropriations Subcommittee on Agriculture. In House debates, these two congressmen assumed an important role in presenting the programs of the Agriculture Committee to their Northern colleagues.[26] The close relationship between city and rural Democrats on farm legislation stands out sharply when it is compared to the Republican record. Stanley Andrews wrote in 1961: "The records will probably show that [Congressman Fiorello] LaGuardia in 1927 and 1928 cast the only Republican city votes in the East for farm price legislation in 30 years." [27]

The public exhortations engaged in by the Democratic leadership in winning urban and industrial votes were most often appeals to party unity or homilies on the expertise of the Agriculture Committee. The debates were punctuated with references to the mutual obligations of sections of the party to each other on matters of concern to each. The city leaders, such as John McCormack of Boston, were fond of pointing out in disinterested fashion that their people had no farms. For example, Abraham Multer of Brooklyn stated on a 1949 bill to establish a rural telephone service: "Despite the fact that there is not a single farm in my district, nor, so far as I know, a single absentee farm owner living there, I will support this bill." [28] The guidelines used by many urban Democrats were perhaps well expressed by Congressman Arthur G. Klein on the 1954 Agriculture Committee program: "So, I have made up my mind, and I believe my colleagues have, those in the Democratic delegation from New York, be-

26. Hence the pastoral Santangelo quotation that opens this chapter. Anfuso served on the Agriculture Committee in the Eighty-fourth and Eighty-fifth Congresses, Santangelo on the Appropriations Subcommittee in the Eighty-sixth and Eighty-seventh Congresses. In the Eighty-eighth Congress, the assignment of Benjamin Rosenthal of Queens to the Agriculture Committee continued the tradition.

27. Andrews, *The Farmer's Dilemma*, p. 98.

28. *Congressional Record*, July 12, 1949, p. 9325.

cause we believe that the men on this Committee on Agriculture are the experts on agricultural matters in this House, and they have voted overwhelmingly for these rigid supports which have been started in a Democratic Congress, and for that reason we are going along with them." [29] (The private exhortations of the party leaders are not documented in the *Congressional Record*. One of the anonymous Democratic congressmen interviewed by Charles Clapp in 1959 did emphasize the importance Speaker Rayburn had attached to putting across party farm policies in 1956: "As a substitute for the caucus the leadership attempts to exert a personal persuasive influence. I have only experienced this on two issues, one of which was the farm bill just prior to the 1956 election. My district opposes the party position on farm policy. The Speaker called me and said, 'This is very vital to the party, particularly with the national election approaching. Can you possibly go along with us?' It was a personal appeal from the Speaker on the day of the vote . . . Friends told me he talked to them also. In effect he buttoned the thing up by that type of personal appeal.")[30]

Democratic farm congressmen from North and South, their policies embraced by the nonfarm majority of the party, had little difficulty during these sixteen years in maintaining respectable party loyalty records on farm issues. The frequency distribution of loyalty scores for congressmen from Democratic farm districts, given in Figure 7, stands in contrast to the Republican distribution in Figure 5. The modal Republican loyalty score lies in the 70's, the median score in the 60's; Democrats from only eight of eighty-three farm districts voted with their party less than 80 percent of the time.

A good argument can be made that the Democratic ap-

29. *Congressional Record,* July 1, 1954, p. 9546.
30. Quoted in Clapp, *The Congressman,* pp. 288–289.

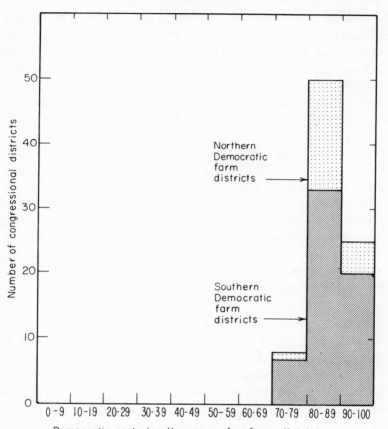

Figure 7. Frequency distribution of party loyalty scores for Democratic farm districts.

proach to agriculture helped to preserve the sometimes tenuous connection between the Northern and Southern wings of the party. So long as the South, or most of it, remained predominantly agricultural, there was good reason for it to remain

Democratic. In Figure 8, frequency distributions of likeness indices derived from the 110 farm votes are presented for, on the one hand, all Southern and all Northern Democrats and, on the other hand, all Southern Democrats and all Republicans. (The South is defined here to include only the eleven Confederate states.) Clearly there was little community of interest uniting Southern farmers and Northern Republicans. (Except on the kinds of issues that produced the very noticeable tails on both frequency distributions in Figure 8. Southerners united with Republicans on questions involving farm labor.) In a special 1950 election, the Republicans contrived to elect a congressman (Ben H. Guill) from the Texas panhandle; in his brief stay in Congress he found it expedient to oppose his party on every recorded farm vote. Among Democrats, however, strong agreement between farm and nonfarm congressmen manifested itself as strong agreement between North and South.

Federal commodity programs, which possess many of the attributes of a leaky tap, have long been the despair of fastidious citizens. Postwar Secretaries of Agriculture of both parties must be numbered among the fastidious. Republican Secretary Ezra Taft Benson sought to overhaul the programs and reduce surpluses by lowering price supports and cutting restrictions on production. Democrats Charles Brannan and Orville Freeman preferred a combination of high price supports and tight production controls. Economists could be found to sanctify the approaches of both parties. Benson meant business; Brannan and Freeman tilted with the problem briefly before surrendering their lances to the House Agriculture Committee. Congress perversely insisted on combining price supports with porous production restrictions, and Congress outlasted all the Secretaries and economists.

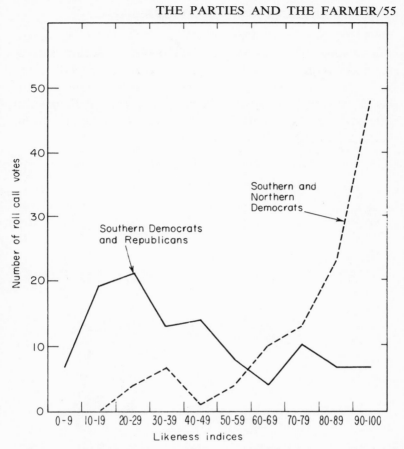

Figure 8. Frequency distributions of likeness indices for Southern Democrats and Republicans and for Southern and Northern Democrats on 110 postwar farm roll calls.

It is important to ask why the farm programs were kept on the books at all. If the actions of congressmen were governed by a crude reading of constituency interest, the farmer would have been abandoned by the federal government some decades ago. The answer, at least in these sixteen postwar years, is that party pressures intervened to magnify the power of the congressional farm minority. In this period of declining farm population, the commodity programs were sustained in the House by the propensity of Democrats from urban and industrial districts to support them by deferring to their rural colleagues. With enough Alfred E. Santangelos behind them, the farmers could still win their battles.

3/THE PARTIES AND THE CITY

"Let me say . . . that I know very little about New York, and if I never know any more I will be just as happy."

— CONGRESSMAN GRAHAM BARDEN
OF NORTH CAROLINA[1]

A NUMBER OF THE NEWER United States Cabinet Departments have been established to serve particular clienteles. Farmers were awarded the Department of Agriculture in 1862, workers and businessmen the separate Departments of Labor and of Commerce in 1913. That by 1962 no Cabinet post had yet been created to handle the problems of city dwellers may be attributed in part to a lingering congressional adherence to rural values, but also in part to the fact that federal involvement in city affairs is a relatively recent development.

This involvement will doubtless grow rather than diminish. It was clear in the Kennedy years, for instance, that the urban transportation snarl was due to receive federal attention. Congress approved in 1961 an experimental program designed to cope with urban juvenile delinquency. The first major federal venture into city affairs, however — the most direct and visible involvement of the New Deal era and beyond — has been in the field of housing. Roll call votes on housing questions thus provide the best key to the attitudes of postwar congressmen toward city problems.

Not all federal housing programs have been controversial and not all have offered special benefits to the cities. The vast

1. *Congressional Record,* March 15, 1948, p. 2875.

insurance operations of the Federal Housing Administration and the Veterans Administration have aided private home-owners in city and country and have received all but universal applause. (A New Deal agency that can evoke statements like one of John Birchite Congressman Edgar Hiestand, "The F.H.A. insurance authorization simply must be renewed," has achieved some sort of ultimate endorsement.)[2] A deep and persistent controversy was touched off, however, with the introduction in the middle 1930's of federal programs designed to provide adequate housing for urban lower income groups not reached by the private construction industry.[3] In the 1947-1962 period, city programs were the source of almost all substantial disagreement on housing legislation. In the immediate postwar years, the most pressing urban problem was a severe housing shortage created in part by wartime population dislocations. Accordingly, city spokesmen were the chief exponents of federal rent control, and continued to be exponents long after rural areas had found controls an annoyance. Of greater duration was the conflict over urban renewal and federally subsidized public housing programs. The bills embodying these programs were complex and contained provisions favoring most sections of the country, but the emphasis was on aid for the cities. Presidents Truman, Eisenhower, and Kennedy all shepherded through Congress significant housing legislation aimed at rendering American cities more habitable.

CITY ISSUES AND CITY DISTRICTS

How, in this period, did the two congressional parties deal with legislation of major concern to the cities? Attention will

2. *Congressional Record,* May 19, 1959, p. 8518.
3. See Timothy L. McDonnell, S.J., *The Wagner Housing Act: A Case Study of the Legislative Process* (Chicago, 1957).

be given here to housing measures voted on in the House of Representatives during the sixteen years. The House contingents of both parties included sizable numbers of city members, and the presumption is that congressmen from opposite parties but from similar city districts were confronted with similar constituency demands. Both parties in the House, then, had to give some consideration to the electoral needs of their city members. Some notion of the ways in which the two parties responded to the problem can be gained by analyzing the relationships which obtained between the city and noncity wings of each party in voting on postwar city issues.

The analysis requires a labeling of a number of congressional districts as "city districts" and a number of House roll call votes as "city votes." The defining of "city districts" is a difficult undertaking, for legal boundaries often do not meaningfully distinguish American cities from their surrounding suburbs. In considering Los Angeles County, for example, it would be hazardous to assign much sociological significance to the pattern of inclusion and exclusion produced by the meandering Los Angeles city limits. The demographer encounters like obstacles in classifying the satellite cities around Boston and New York. In an effort to supply a sensible distinction between "city districts" and "noncity districts," and at the same time to include as "city districts" those areas most likely to have favored postwar housing legislation, a two-pronged definition of "city districts" has been chosen here. First, a 1962 *Congressional Quarterly* study, in which district populations are broken down according to their "rural," "urban," and "suburban" percentages, has been used to eliminate from consideration districts 50 percent or more rural.[4] Second,

___

4. *Congressional Quarterly Weekly Report,* February 2, 1962. Population data from the 1960 Census are used, but the district boundaries are those not yet affected by the census returns. *Congressional Quarterly* fol-

districts with combined "urban" and "suburban" populations of more than 50 percent have been subjected to a further test. An owner occupancy index taken from the *Congressional District Data Book* has been used to exclude from consideration districts with more than 66.6 percent of dwelling units owned by occupants.[5] The argument is that metropolitan districts with minimal rental occupancy merit classification as suburban, regardless of their location inside or outside city boundaries. The residual "city districts" to be used in this study are those districts less than one-half "rural," and with fewer than two-thirds of their dwelling units owned by occupants. (In the following pages, these districts will be referred to as "city districts" and their congressmen as "city congressmen." Districts not satisfying the two qualifications, whether they were rural or suburban in complexion, will be referred to simply as "noncity districts" and their congressmen as "noncity congressmen.")

The chief effects of this employment of two separate qualifications in arriving at a suitable definition of "city districts" are (1) an inclusion here of some districts classified by *Congressional Quarterly* as predominantly "suburban," and (2) an elimination of some districts classified by *Congressional Quarterly* as predominantly "urban." For example, the Eighth Massachusetts district, which embraced Everett, Malden, Medford, and part of Somerville, but which is categorized by *Congressional Quarterly* as 97.1 percent "suburban," is included here as a "city district" because of its low (59.7 percent) ownership occupancy rate. On the other hand, the Twenty-first California district, which took in the northern

---

lows, with some deviations, the Census Bureau definitions of "urban," "suburban," and "rural."

5. U.S. Bureau of the Census, *Congressional District Data Book, Districts of the 87th Congress* (Washington, D.C., 1961). Occupancy figures are taken from 1960 census data.

half of Los Angeles County, but most of whose people lived within the city limits, is counted here as a "noncity district" because of its high (71.4 percent) ownership occupancy rate. An index that labels Torbert Macdonald (D. Massachusetts 8) rather than Edgar Hiestand (R. California 21) a "city congressman" makes at least as much sense as one that does the reverse.

In 1961, there were 140 Congressmen from what have been called "city districts." [6] Fifty-eight of the districts lay in the Northeastern urban belt running from Boston to Washington, 23 in cities on the Great Lakes, 16 in California, 20 in the South, the rest in scattered cities. Thirty-five of the districts were served in 1961 by Republicans, 105 by Democrats. The Republicans were not very successful in winning city districts in the postwar years, and, as the figures from the Eighty-seventh Congress presented in Table 8 indicate, the party had an especially difficult time in districts with very high rates of rental occupancy of dwelling units. In 1961, only eleven of fifty-seven congressmen from city districts with less than 50 percent of ownership occupancy were Republicans, and in most of these eleven cases the districts had been constructed with care by Republican state legislatures.

The next requirement here is a number of House roll call votes that can be called "city votes." Fifty roll calls and the list of signatures on one House discharge petition have been

6. The *Congressional Quarterly Weekly Report*'s urbanism figures and the Census Bureau's ownership occupancy data both apply to congressional districts existent between 1953 and 1962. In this chapter, attention will be devoted to roll call votes ranging back to 1947. In defining "city districts" existent in the 1947–1952 period, it has been assumed that "city districts" not subjected to boundary changes were "city districts" both before and after the 1950 Census and resultant reapportionment. Where there were boundary changes a very murky problem arises, for there is an impressive lack of data on the intracounty congressional districts of earlier years. Pre-1952 districts have been counted as "city districts" if they covered roughly the same territory covered by post-1952 "city districts."

TABLE 8. Percentage of dwelling units occupied by owners in city districts served by Democrats and Republicans, Eighty-seventh Congress, 1961–1962

Percentage of owner occupancy of dwelling units in districts	Districts held by Democrats	Districts held by Republicans
0.0–9.9	9	1[a]
10.0–19.9	4	0
20.0–29.9	15	1[b]
30.0–39.9	5	3[c]
40.0–49.9	13	6[d]
50.0–59.9	25	9
60.0–66.7	34	15
Total	105	35

[a] Lindsay (Manhattan).
[b] McDonough (Los Angeles).
[c] Lipscomb (Los Angeles); Curtis (Boston); Fino (Bronx).
[d] Scherer (Cincinnati); Ray (Staten Island-Brooklyn); Bell (Los Angeles); Mailliard (San Francisco); Judd (Minneapolis); Wallhauser (Newark).

selected from the records of the postwar era. (The record of preferences on the discharge petition, the instrument employed in an abortive attempt to pry the Taft-Ellender-Wagner housing bill from committee in 1948, will, for convenience, be treated and referred to as a roll call vote. Failure to sign the petition is construed as disapproval of the bill. There are obvious dangers in handling a discharge petition in this fashion, but no other record of views on housing legislation in the Eightieth Congress is available.) Included in the total are votes on the authorization of federal pilot projects to combat urban juvenile delinquency (1961) and on the attempted establishment of a Department of Urban Affairs and Housing (1962). Almost all the roll calls, however, were on federal housing programs of impact in the cities — that is, votes on federal rent control and on authorization of and appropriations for urban renewal and subsidized public housing programs. Housing votes on such questions as F.H.A. interest rates have been excluded from consideration. (That federal intervention in housing matters in this period was both more popular and more far-reaching in the city than in the country is an unassailable fact. The disparity in public favor did not derive, however, from a like disparity in the quality of existent housing. In 1960, according to census figures, only 18 percent of households in standard metropolitan statistical areas [these areas include suburbs] lived in units structurally unsound or without standard plumbing facilities. Thirty-seven percent of rural households were so afflicted. There was doubtless a difference between city and country in the perception of housing problems, or in the perception of political devices for improving housing quality.)[7]

For purposes of demonstration in the following analysis, the fifty-one "city votes" will at times be divided into four separate blocks. The first block includes seventeen votes on rent control in the 1947–1952 period and can reasonably be set apart. The second block comprises twelve votes on housing during the Truman Administration and the 1948 discharge petition. In these years the focus was on the enactment of the ambitious Wagner-Ellender-Taft (or Taft-Ellender-Wagner) housing program, the core of which was approved by Congress in 1949. The third block includes nine votes from the 1953–

7. The statistics were cited in *Review of Federal Housing Programs,* p. 16, appendix to Senate Committee on Banking and Currency, 87th Congress, 1st Sess., *Hearings on Various Bills to Amend the Federal Housing Laws.* It should be added that the "city districts" defined above do not constitute an exhaustive list of congressional districts which benefited from federal housing programs. For example, the cities of Harrisburg and Chattanooga, though located in districts classified by *Congressional Quarterly Weekly Report* as over 50 percent rural, profited handsomely from the urban renewal program. The geography of federal housing expenditures through the 1950's is explored in *Review of Federal Housing Programs,* pp. 93–96.

1958 period. With Congress and the President more conservative, many of the votes were on efforts to sustain the public housing program that had been authorized in 1949. The fourth block includes twelve votes from the 1959–1962 period. An injection of Northern Democrats into Congress in 1959 stimulated attempts to enact a more sweeping urban renewal program, but this time with less emphasis on subsidized public housing. President Eisenhower vetoed two costly Democratic housing bills in 1959, but President Kennedy signed one into law in 1961.

If cities were the beneficiaries of federal housing programs, it is reasonable to expect that city congressmen should have demonstrated greater unity than noncity congressmen in voting on them. The figures in Table 9 indicate that this was

TABLE 9. Mean cohesion of city and noncity congressmen on four sets of postwar city roll calls

	17 votes on rent control, 1947–1952	13 votes on housing, 1947–1952	9 votes on housing, 1953–1958	12 votes on housing and other city issues, 1959–1962
All city	51	47	37	49
All noncity	18	33	29	16

indeed the tendency, although the high cohesion of city congressmen can be attributed in good part to the heavy Democratic imbalance among city members. Nevertheless, the low cohesion of noncity congressmen suggests that housing programs — programs favoring the cities — were passed because noncity congressmen did not unite in opposing them.

An examination of party operations can shed light upon questions raised by the data in Table 9.

PARTY PRESSURES

Each party in the postwar House of Representatives embraced congressmen from both city and country. If bipartisan blocs of city and of noncity congressmen did not each rally together to oppose one another on expensive city legislation, the suspicion immediately arises that party pressures may have intervened to deflect congressmen from an untrammeled reflection of constituency interest. On farm legislation, it was found that party pressures flowed in opposite directions. The same tests will be applied here to detect whether city programs were championed by one party and opposed by the other. With cohesion indices and the voting records of party leaders as tools, the relations between city and noncity wings of each party on city votes will be plumbed.

If there existed a directional difference in party pressures, it should be detectable in cohesion data. The assumption, once again, is that a congressional bloc buffeted by coinciding constituency and party pressures will normally demonstrate a higher degree of unity than a bloc buffeted by conflicting pressures. In Figure 9, frequency distributions of cohesion indices on the fifty-one postwar city votes are presented for the city and noncity branches of each party. The contrast between the parties is striking. Republican noncity congressmen were clearly more united on housing issues than their Democratic counterparts. Among city congressmen, however, the modal cohesion index of Democrats is in the 80's, and of the Republicans down in the 40's. The figures suggest that the Democrats espoused housing policies popular among their city

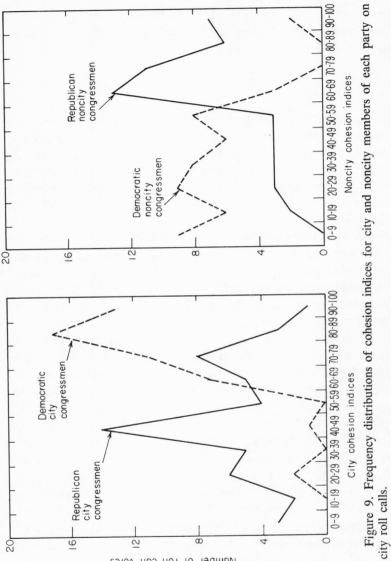

Figure 9. Frequency distributions of cohesion indices for city and noncity members of each party on city roll calls.

members and sought support for them among their noncity members. The indication is that the Republicans adopted policies popular in the country but had some difficulty in selling them to their congressmen most directly concerned with housing problems.

Corroborating evidence of the contrasting party approaches is provided in the voting records of elected party leaders (the two top voting officials in each party) on city questions. The leaders of a party may be assumed to be bolstering the position of one bloc in a party rather than another if their recorded stand on an issue is that of a significantly higher proportion of the members of the former than of the latter. The two blocs in question here are the city and noncity segments of each party. City and noncity Republicans differed significantly on thirty of the fifty-one roll calls of the period, city and noncity Democrats on forty-six. (The chi square test has been used again here, with significance at the .05 level.) Republican city and country wings did disagree less consistently then the Democratic wings, but, when disagreements occurred, Republican leaders almost always reinforced the positions of their noncity members, Democratic leaders the positions of their city people. Exhibited below are figures showing respectively the number of times the leaders of each party favored the city position, were themselves divided, and favored the noncity position.

| Republicans | 4 | 4 | 22 |
| Democrats | 44 | 1 | 1 |

The cohesion figures and leadership voting records present a picture of Democratic city and Republican noncity congressmen wafted by coinciding party and constituency pressures, but of Democratic noncity and Republican city congressmen torn by conflicting pressures. In other words, the figures suggest that party pressures on city issues did flow in opposite directions. The Democrats had succeeded in these years in establishing themselves not only as the party of the farmer but as the party of the city dweller — an extraordinary accomplishment.

In fact, on all the controversial housing issues of this period — on rent control, on public housing, on urban renewal — House Democratic leaders did embrace the positions of the city wing of their party. Sam Rayburn and Carl Albert, party spokesmen from Arcadian districts in Texas and Oklahoma, were as consistent in their advocacy of city programs as John McCormack of Boston. House Republican leaders, with but one major blemish on their record, led the forces opposing city positions in all postwar housing controversies. The blemish was the party's endorsement of rent control in the Eightieth Congress; Republican leaders secured passage of rent legislation denounced as inadequate by most Democrats and as unnecessary by many Republicans.

For House Republicans, the coming of the Eisenhower Administration provided certain embarrassments. The most fiercely contested provision of the Housing Act of 1949 was one authorizing construction of 810,000 public housing units over a six-year period. Republican leaders viewed the program as an abomination and, in succeeding years, assaulted it through the appropriations process. President Eisenhower, however, endorsed a modest version of the very same program in 1954. Party members in the House responded by voting three to one against the President's proposal; Majority Leader Charles Halleck, though visibly distressed by Eisenhower's eccentricity, sided with the President and with the party minority.[8]

To say, however, that the Republicans assumed an anticity position on all controversial housing issues in these years is not to say that the party opposed all housing programs aiding

8. *Congressional Record,* April 1 and 2, 1954, pp. 4361–4489.

the cities, nor that party policy remained fixed after 1947. In fact, the congressional consensus on housing matters surely moved toward a greater acceptance of urban renewal programs. President Eisenhower, by winning general Republican support for urban renewal, gave the consensus a push forward. But he did not change the relative positions of the parties. Where Democrats and Republicans of this sixteen-year period chose to conflict on housing questions, and where they therefore chose to distinguish their respective public images, Democrats spoke for the city and Republicans for the country.

THE REPUBLICANS

A sizable proportion of Republican city congressmen, most notably those from Los Angeles, found party housing policies quite congenial. (Public housing and urban renewal programs were predictably more popular in old Eastern cities than in the newer cities of the Southwest.) Throughout the postwar years, however, a number of city Republicans rejected the party position as untenable and voted frequently with the Democrats. The decision to rebel could be a difficult one to make. As Congressman John Lindsay of Manhattan remarked in 1961, in discussing his previous votes for public housing, "At times I assure my friends on the Democratic side that it was not easy, because there is some disagreement on my side of the aisle on the public housing question." [9] Hoary ideological tenets of the party had to be called into question, for Republican dislike of public housing was probably more deep-seated than party distaste for the more traditional farm subsidies. Congressmen Claude Bakewell of St. Louis and Richard Welch of San Francisco, supporters of the housing programs of the late 1940's, rose in the House to express annoyance at persistent

9. *Congressional Record,* June 22, 1961, p. 11134.

charges — most of them from their own party — that the programs were socialistic.[10]

City Republicans often outlined their constituency problems in House debates. In 1950, by which time the party had developed a strong aversion to federal rent control, Congressman Edgar Jonas described conditions in Chicago and concluded, "I will have to support some kind of rent-control legislation . . ." [11] In 1955, Congressman Frederic Coudert, Jr. of Manhattan, a conservative on many issues, justified his vote for public housing in what can best be described as a plaintive apology to the Republican leadership: "Mr. Speaker, I rise with the utmost reluctance when it means expressing disagreement with the distinguished gentleman from Michigan [Jesse Wolcott, ranking Republican on the Banking and Currency Committee — the committee that handles housing legislation], for whom I have the highest regard and whom I have followed through the years. This is a case, however, where I am forced by circumstances to disagree with him and rise in support of this conference report. I do it because, much as I regret it, I am forced to recognize the desperate situation of housing in the great city of New York, a part of which I have the honor to represent." [12] Congressman Jacob Javits of Manhattan, while in the House the most vocal of the liberal Republicans, argued persistently that housing legislation was and should be a bipartisan undertaking. Just after the 1948 election, Javits spoke for rent control in the name of "some 70 Republican Members who came from big cities and who are not here today. Those men want to run again, they want to be elected, and I think we on our side have to give some thought to their situation." [13]

10. *Congressional Record,* June 18, 1948, p. 8880; June 22, 1949, p. 8166.
11. *Congressional Record,* June 13, 1950, p. 8522.
12. *Congressional Record,* August 2, 1955, p. 12980.
13. *Congressional Record,* March 11, 1949, p. 2286.

Very little thought was given to their situation, and when put in historical perspective the Republican success in city districts in 1946 — in the "meat shortage election" — stands out as an aberration. (Carrying all six districts in Philadelphia must have required favorable circumstances just short of divine intervention.) Where city districts were subsequently held by the party, the price of victory was often an adherence by their congressmen to Democratic policy positions. A frequency distribution of party loyalty scores for Republican city districts is presented in Figure 10. (As in the farm analysis, each loyalty score is based not on the record of an individual congressman but on the record of all congressmen of one party serving a postwar district if they served it in three or more Congresses of the eight.) The median score is in the 70's, but the lower scores are well scattered. There existed no "bloc" of deviant city Republicans, but party ties for some individuals were, at best, tenuous. A list of twenty-five city districts whose Republican congressmen were least loyal on city issues is given in Table 10. (In this and succeeding tables, where a district's number was changed after the 1950 Census both numbers are given.) Though a number of Midwestern and Western districts appear, nine of the districts were in the state of New York and eighteen in the Northeast.

Differences in the behavior of Republican city congressmen should be traceable, to a degree, to differences in the nature of their districts. There is good reason to expect that the party loyalty of city Republicans should have tailed off, on the one hand, in districts with low proportions of ownership occupancy of dwelling units and, on the other hand, in districts where the threat of Democratic victory was clear and present. In Table 11, a cross-tabulation of district loyalty scores is presented, the variables being the ownership occupancy percentage in each district and the median Republican percentage of the two-

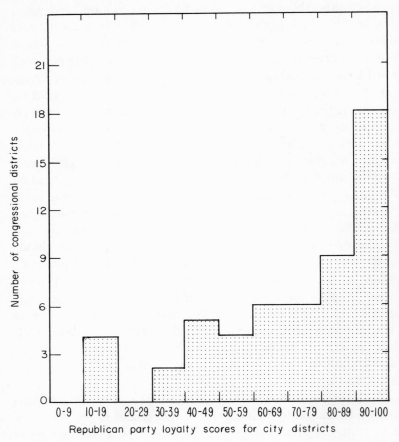

Figure 10. Frequency distribution of party loyalty scores for Republican city districts.

party vote in all regular postwar elections won by Republican congressional candidates in each district.

The data in the cells in Table 11 are thin, but one fairly persuasive pattern emerges. In all three groupings of districts

TABLE 10. City districts whose Republican congressmen ranked lowest
in party loyalty on city issues, 1947–1962

District	Cities partly or wholly represented	Congressmen	No. of recorded votes of all district congressmen	Party loyalty score for all congressmen serving each district
N.Y. 25	Bronx	Fino	21	10
N.Y. 12	Brooklyn	Dorn	15	13
N.Y. 21	Manhattan	Javits	32	16
N.J. 8	Paterson	Canfield	41	17
N.J. 6	Elizabeth	Case, Dwyer	43	30
N.J. 12	Newark	Kean, Wallhauser	50	34
Cal. 4	San Francisco	Mailliard	20	40
N.Y. 17	Manhattan	Coudert, Lindsay	48	42
Conn. 4	Bridgeport	Lodge, Morano	42	43
Pa. 3	Philadelphia	(Hardie) Scott	29	45
Ore. 3	Portland	Angell	33	48
Minn. 5	Minneapolis	Judd	50	52
Ill. 12	Chicago	Jonas	23	52
Conn. 3	New Haven	Foote, Cretella	17	53
N.Y. 3, 4	Queens	Latham, Halpern	49	59
Pa. 10	Scranton	Scoblick, Carrigg, Scranton	22	64
Wis. 5	Milwaukee	Kersten	14	64
Ky. 3	Louisville	Morton, Robsion	31	65
Conn. AL	Hartford, New Haven, Bridgeport	Sadlak	36	67
Mass. 10	Boston	Herter, Curtis	48	67
Ohio 22	Cleveland	(Frances) Bolton	51	69
N.Y. 43, 41	Buffalo	Elsaesser, Radwan	20	70
N.Y. 28, 26	New Rochelle, White Plains	Gamble, Dooley	49	76
N.Y. 36, 35	Syracuse	Riehlman	48	77
N.Y. 40, 38	Rochester	Keating, Weis	49	78

according to levels of party electoral strength, Republican
congressmen serving districts with low ownership occupancy
percentages (under 50 percent) tended to be less faithful to
the party than their colleagues from districts with more home-
owners. In other words, Republicans from the core areas of

TABLE 11. Party loyalty of Republican city congressmen, 1947–1962, as a function of district ownership occupancy percentage and district partisan balance[a]

	Median Republican electoral percentage			Mean party loyalty
	51.6–55.4	55.7–59.0	59.3–70.7	
Owner occupancy percentage: 0.0–49.9	$(N = 6)$[b] 63	$(N = 6)$ 53	$(N = 5)$ 63	59
Owner occupancy percentage: 50.0–59.9	$(N = 6)$ 83	$(N = 3)$ 83	$(N = 7)$ 76	80
Owner occupancy percentage: 60.0–66.7	$(N = 6)$ 72	$(N = 8)$ 70	$(N = 6)$ 86	76
Mean party loyalty	73	66	76	
Proportion of seats still in Republican hands after 1962 election	33.3	61.1	83.3	

[a] Fifty-three districts have been ranked in three sets according to their ownership occupancy percentages and also according to their electoral percentages, the consequent cross-tabulation thus producing nine cells. The three sets of districts ranked by electoral percentage include equal numbers (18-17-18) of districts. The three sets ranked by ownership occupancy percentage include districts with percentages ranging respectively from 0.0 to 49.9, from 50.0 to 59.9, and from 60.0 to 66.7. Data are included for districts which elected Republicans to at least three Congresses and whose congressmen cast at least ten "city votes" in the House. In the determination of the median Republican election percentages, data from uncontested elections were not considered.

[b] "N" in each of the nine cells refers to the number of districts satisfying the requisite electoral and occupancy criteria, and hence the number for which the loyalty score in each cell has been calculated.

cities — where home ownership is rare — bolted the party more often on housing issues regardless of the "safeness" of their districts.

No correlation appears in Table 11, however, between Republican electoral strength in city districts and the party loyalty on city issues of their Republican congressmen. It does not seem to have been fear of defeat that nudged Republicans into heresy. There is reason to believe, however, that the data in the table conceal the workings of a number of factors, that there really was some relationship between party loyalty and party electoral strength. In the first place, there was a tendency for Republicans from city districts where the secular electoral trend has been Republican (as in Phoenix and Dallas) to demonstrate greater party fidelity than those from districts where the secular trend has been Democratic (as in Portland, Ore., Milwaukee, and Philadelphia). Median Republican electoral percentages do not distinguish these two types of districts.

In the second place, it is instructive to note that, although the districts in Table 11 of lowest median Republican percentage chose congressmen rather loyal to the party, the party was not able to hold very many of these districts with any consistency. Of these eighteen districts won by Republicans at least three times, only six were in Republican hands after the 1962 election. It may be that, in some cities, the attitudes of Republican activists foreclosed nomination of liberal Republicans who could compete successfully in the long run with Democratic opponents. New York City consistently sustained a number of liberal Republicans in Congress; Chicago often sent conservative Republicans to Congress by narrow margins in good Republican years but then threw them out of office in succeeding elections. Among the districts with low median Republican electoral percentages are two that had been consistently Republican until the middle 1950's. Their congressmen, Angier Goodwin (Massachusetts 8, Malden, Somerville, et al.) and John Allen (California 7, Oakland), both conservatives with high party loyalty scores on city questions, lost their seats to the Democrats respectively in 1954 and 1958. Both men broke career records to vote with the Democrats on housing in the congressional sessions immediately preceding their electoral defeats, but their conversions may have come too late.

A temporary conversion of Republican William Hess of Cincinnati was apparently inspired by electoral defeat. Hess followed the party line in the Eightieth Congress but lost his seat in the 1948 election. He won narrowly in 1950, voted three times with the Democrats on public housing in the Eighty-second Congress, but voted with his party on housing matters in the four succeeding Congresses after his election margins had returned to normal.

In the third place, some Republican congressmen unquestionably built safe city districts for themselves by convincing their constituents that they were not regular Republicans. Hence the high Republican electoral percentages in some districts whose congressmen scored low in party loyalty may be attributable to the political attractiveness of the congressmen rather than of their party. The proposition can be tested by observing what happened to Republican electoral percentages in districts when party congressmen of differing loyalty records retired, died, or were replaced by other Republican nominees. In Table 12, thirty-seven city districts, in each of which the party nomination passed at some time in the postwar period from a Republican who was serving or had served in Congress to a Republican newcomer, have been ranked in four sets according to the personal loyalty records of the retiring congressmen. For each district, the difference between the mean two-party electoral percentage of the retiring congressman in his last two election attempts and the two-party electoral percentage of the successor nominee has been calculated. For each of the four sets of districts in Table 12, a median change in Republican electoral percentage has been determined. The common result of a switch in congressional nominees is, of course, a marginal drop in party electoral strength. The figures in Table 12 indicate, however, that Republican losses in percentage were most severe in city districts where retiring con-

TABLE 12. Relation between party loyalty records of retiring Republican city congressmen and subsequent changes in Republican electoral strength, 1947–1962[a]

	Median change in Republican percentage of two-party vote
First quartile: 10 retiring congressmen, with party loyalty scores ranging from 8 to 53	− 7.2
Second quartile: 9 retiring congressmen, with party loyalty scores ranging from 54 to 76	− 3.1
Third quartile: 9 retiring congressmen, with party loyalty scores ranging from 77 to 91	− 2.4
Fourth quartile: 9 retiring congressmen, with party loyalty scores ranging from 91 to 100	− 0.4

[a] A district is included here if its retiring congressman served in at least two Congresses and voted on at least ten city roll calls. Two districts (Conn. 4 and N.Y. 26), in each of which there were two Republican "transitions" in the postwar years, are counted twice in the table. The focus here is on the change from the man with a congressional voting record to the newcomer, so the critical switch of nominees may have taken place after the former had already lost his seat. Antoni Sadlak (Conn. AL), for instance, was turned out of office in the 1958 election, ran again unsuccessfully in 1960, and was replaced by another Republican nominee in 1962; the variation in Republican electoral percentage to be considered is that between 1960 and 1962. In the determination of electoral percentages for this table, data from uncontested elections have not been included.

gressmen had been disloyal to the party on city questions. When Jacob Javits (New York 21) left his Manhattan district in 1954, the Republican share of the two-party vote plummeted 33.2 percent. The 1954 retirement of Clifford Case (New Jersey 6, Elizabeth) precipitated a Republican loss of 20.5 percent. The death of Richard Welch of San Francisco (California 5) converted his seat from uncontested Republican in 1948 to uncontested Democratic in 1950. In a number of districts, notably those of Javits, Welch, Hardie Scott (Pennsylvania 3, Philadelphia), Homer Angell (Oregon 3, Portland), Edmund Radwan (New York 41, Buffalo), and Gordon Canfield (New Jersey 8, Paterson), the Republicans had no real chance of electing congressmen after the retirement from office of popular but independent-minded party incumbents.

The data in Table 11 indicated that there was no relationship between the party loyalty of postwar city Republicans and the "safeness" of their seats, that, in other words, party loyalty did not decline among congressmen seemingly most vulnerable to defeat. In fact, the table masks a number of factors. Most city Republicans with low median electoral percentages but high party loyalty scores were not able to keep their seats, and some of those who succeeded were assisted by beneficent secular electoral trends. City Republicans with high median electoral percentages but low party loyalty scores had discovered an important fact of political life: one of the best ways for a Republican to construct a safe seat in a city area was to vote with the Democrats on city questions.

THE DEMOCRATS

If many Republicans serving city districts had to do violence to party principles, Democratic city congressmen, in responding to constituency demands, could reflect happily upon the orthodoxy of their actions. A frequency distribution of party loyalty scores for postwar Democratic congressmen serving each city district is presented in Figure 11. (In Figure 11 and in succeeding tables and figures, the South — unless otherwise indicated — will be taken to include only the eleven Confederate states, the North the remaining non-Confederate states.) An overwhelming majority of Democratic city districts elected

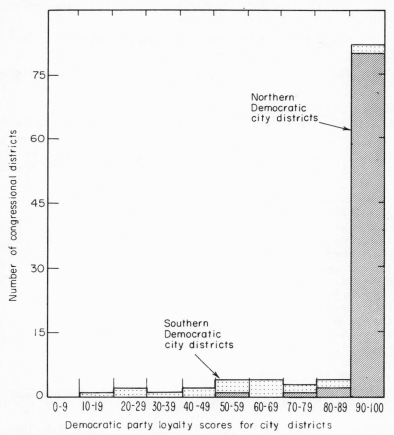

Figure 11. Frequency distribution of party loyalty scores for Democratic city districts.

congressmen who voted with a party majority on over 90 percent of city issues. What made possible the fidelity of city Democrats was, of course, the willingness of Democratic congressmen from noncity areas to support city programs. The flow of party pressures rendered the position of the city minority the position of a party majority.

Among Democrats from districts outside the eleven Confederate states, support for party housing policies was close to monolithic. In Table 13, mean cohesion indices for all North-

TABLE 13. Solidarity of Northern Democrats on city issues

	17 votes on rent control, 1947–1952	13 votes on housing, 1947–1952	9 votes on housing, 1953–1958	12 votes on housing and other city issues, 1959–1962
Mean cohesion of all Northern Democratic congressmen	84	88	92	90
Mean likeness indices for Northern city and Northern noncity Democratic congressmen	92	94	95	94

ern Democrats and mean likeness indices for Northern city and Northern noncity Democrats are presented for the four sets of postwar city roll calls. Generous assistance was given to urban Democrats by their colleagues from the mountain states, from Midwestern farm areas, from scattered blue collar districts, and from the border states.

A good deal less assistance was forthcoming from the South. The low cohesion on city issues of the entire noncity wing of the Democratic party, pointed to earlier in Figure 9, is attributable to Southern apostasy. With most Southern Democrats representing agricultural areas, the House debates on housing were characterized by repeated appeals from Northern city Democrats for intraparty reciprocity. Congressmen who served as brokers for farm interests, such as Alfred Santangelo of Manhattan, faced in the other direction: "I say to you Members from the farm States whom we have supported time and time again that this policy of Government aid is a two-way street. We want you to support us to the same extent we supported you." [14] The statement of Graham Barden that opens this chapter — an expression of total unconcern about New York problems — evoked a long and spirited lecture by New York Congressman Walter Lynch on what it meant to be a Democrat. [15] But such appeals fell upon many deaf ears. A good many Southerners agreed with the sentiments of Congressman William Colmer of Mississippi on public housing: "It strikes at the very bulwark of the Republic. It is un-American. It is socialistic in the truest sense of the word." [16] And, whereas city Democrats shied away from vocal opposition to party farm policies, Southern Democrats as often as not took the lead in offering crippling amendments to Democratic housing bills. The likeness figures in Figure 12 reveal that Southern Democratic congressmen, taken as a whole, agreed more closely with Republicans than with Northern Democrats on housing matters.

There were, however, Southerners and Southerners. For years Senator John Sparkman and Congressman Albert Rains, both of Alabama, led liberal forces in congressional campaigns for federal housing legislation. The loyalty scores of Southern city congressmen on city issues, given in Figure 11, cover a wide spectrum; Congressmen James C. Davis of Atlanta and Hale Boggs of New Orleans — both in Congress throughout

14. *Congressional Record*, May 21, 1959, p. 8829.
15. *Congressional Record*, March 15, 1948, pp. 2875–2876.
16. *Congressional Record*, April 2, 1954, p. 4464.

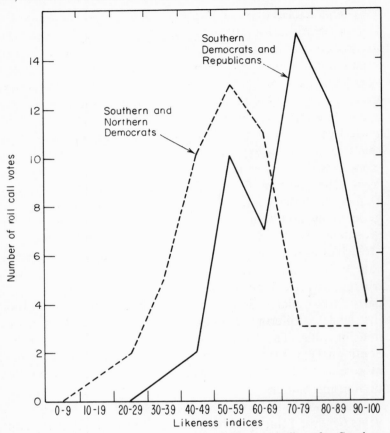

Figure 12. Frequency distributions of likeness indices for Southern Democrats and Republicans and for Southern and Northern Democrats on 51 postwar city roll calls.

the eight postwar sessions — voted with the party respectively 14 percent and 92 percent of the time. The random scattering of the city congressmen's loyalty scores is doubtless traceable in good measure to the fact that lower income groups in Southern cities — less involved in politics than corresponding Northerners — exerted no consistent pressure for liberal legislation.[17] Loyalty records of rural Southern congressmen, however, also range across the spectrum.

On balance, there was a discernible relationship between the attitudes of Southern congressmen on housing issues and the rural-urban complexion of their districts. In Table 14, mean

TABLE 14. Party loyalty of Southern Democratic congressmen on city issues, 1947–1962, as a function of district "rural" percentage[a]

	Percentage "rural" population in districts			
	0.0–24.9	25.0–49.9	50.0–74.9	75.0–100.0
Mean party loyalty scores for districts	60	58	51	48
Number of districts	(13)	(9)	(20)	(55)

Source: The "rural" percentages were taken from the study in *Congressional Quarterly Weekly Report*, February 2, 1962. Areas not counted as "rural" are classified by *Congressional Quarterly* as either "urban" or "suburban."

[a] In preceding pages, party loyalty scores have been calculated for city districts (1) which elected members of a party to at least three postwar Congresses, and (2) whose congressmen of that party voted on at least ten city roll calls. The object has been to include as many districts as possible in the loyalty analysis. In this table, loyalty scores are included for 97 Southern districts that elected Democrats to at least five postwar Congresses. (Since Sam Rayburn voted infrequently, no data are included for his Fourth Texas district.) Consistent Democratic domination of the overwhelming majority of Southern districts makes possible the more stringent time requirement, and the elimination of districts that elected Democrats to fewer than five Congresses renders the district loyalty scores for the longer periods more directly comparable.

loyalty scores are given for congressmen serving sets of districts ranked according to the percentages of their populations inhabiting "rural" areas. Southern congressmen representing

17. See V. O. Key, Jr., *Southern Politics in State and Nation* (New York, 1949), chap. xxiv, and Donald R. Matthews and James W. Prothro, "Social and Economic Factors and Negro Voter Registration in the South," *American Political Science Review,* 57:24–44 (March 1963).

urban constituents were marginally more faithful to the party on housing issues than those serving rural constituents.

The student of Southern politics is forewarned that the basic division on most political questions has been between whites inside and outside the Black Belt.[18] The conservatism of Black Belt whites, the product of an economics based on Negro labor and a politics based on Negro disfranchisement, has contrasted with the more liberal outlook of whites in the mountain and Piedmont regions where Negroes have been few. In a search for demographic correlates of congressional behavior on housing questions, an introduction of data ranking Southern districts according to percentage Negro population produces interesting results.[19] Figure 13 shows the relationship between the party loyalty of Southern congressmen on city issues and the percentage "rural" population of their districts, but with percentage Negro population in the districts held constant. (The Figure is based on data for all Southern Democratic districts except those in Texas; the conventional Southern cleavage between Black Belt and upland whites has not existed in Texas, and the inclusion here of data for a large number of Texas districts would obscure the results.) The tendency in these years was for Southern congressmen serving cities to support party housing policies with about equal fervor regardless of the racial composition of their districts. A good many federal housing projects were, of course, segregated. Among Southern rural congressmen, however, the traditional ideological cleavage appears. Rural Democrats from heavily white areas gave substantially more support to the party on city

18. See Key, *Southern Politics in State and Nation.*
19. *Congressional Quarterly Weekly Report,* March 30, 1962, gives figures for each congressional district showing "nonwhite" population as a percentage of total district population. 1960 census figures are used. In considering Southern districts, "nonwhite" can be read to mean "Negro."

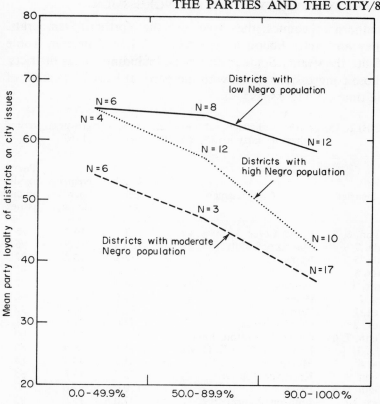

Figure 13. Party loyalty of Southern Democratic congressmen on city issues as a function of district "rural" percentage and district Negro percentage. Figures are included for districts that elected Democrats to at least five postwar Congresses.

issues than their rural colleagues from the Black Belt. (A Republican congressman in the Clapp study pinned a label on some of the former: "There are a group of Southerners I call TVA Southerners. Those in the TVA area don't vote with their

Southern colleagues: they vote with the Northern Democrats. They are pretty liberal all the way.")[20] Listed here in Table 15 are the twenty Southern districts, including Texas districts, whose congressmen voted with the party at least 75 percent of the time on city issues.

TABLE 15. Southern districts whose Democratic congressmen scored highest in party loyalty on city issues, 1947–1962

District	Congressmen	Rural per-centage	Negro per-centage	Party loyalty on city issues
Tenn. 6, 5	Priest, Loser	13.3	19.2	96
Ala. 7	Manasco, Elliott	100.0	9.9	95
Ala. 5	Rains	77.5	15.8	92
Ala. 8	Jones	80.4	16.0	92
Ark. 3	Trimble	80.0	2.3	92
La. 2	Boggs	14.1	31.0	92
Tex. 1	Patman	86.6	26.7	92
Tex. 2	Combs, Brooks	44.0	31.6	91
Tenn. 7, 6	Courtney, Sutton, Bass	100.0	13.0	90
Ga. 7	Lanham, Mitchell, Davis	95.5	8.8	88
La. 6	Morrison	63.9	35.4	88
Tenn. 3	Kefauver, Frazier	55.2	13.3	85
Tenn. 5, 4	Evins	100.0	7.0	83
Tex. 10	Johnson, Thornberry	47.0	15.0	83
Tenn. 9, 8	Cooper, Everett	100.0	26.3	82
Va. 9	Flannagan, Fugate, Jennings	100.0	2.7	81
Tenn. 10, 9	Davis	13.2	36.4	80
Ala. 9	Battle, Huddleston	17.9	34.6	79
Ga. 10	Brown, Stephens	68.2	33.1	78
Ala. 4	Hobbs, Roberts	100.0	31.7	77

The mixed records of Southern Democrats in the 1947–1962 period should not cloud the fact that the outlook of Northern city Democrats on city questions was clearly domi-

20. Quoted in Clapp, *The Congressman*, p. 323.

nant within the party. Democratic housing policies won the support of almost all Northern Democratic congressmen and of a substantial proportion of Southerners. The position of a majority of city Democrats was also the position of a majority of noncity Democrats on forty-eight of the fifty-one postwar city votes.

Congressman Brent Spence of Kentucky, Democratic Chairman of the House Banking and Currency Committee throughout most of this period, once explained housing politics in the following fashion: "Those who do not need public housing, and never see it, have a settled aversion to it. But Members who come from Districts that need it are for it." [21] The statement, a weary reflection on the wrongheadedness of rural elements in both parties, happens not to have been true. The United States Congress would be a far different place if its members approached legislation with such narrow calculations. Though it would be foolish to deny that postwar housing programs struck a more responsive chord among city congressmen than among their rural colleagues, data have been marshaled to show that, on city issues, party was as important as constituency in explaining the positions of congressmen and the outcomes of legislative struggles.

In housing matters as in farm matters, Republican and Democratic pressures flowed in opposite directions. In both cases, Democrats bolstered the positions of their congressmen from "interested" districts and Republicans placed party weight behind their congressmen from relatively "indifferent" districts. As a result, farm and city Democrats displayed extraordinary unity on issues of district relevance, but farm and city Republicans were divided. On both sets of issues, "indifferent" Democrats were less united than their "interested" brethren, "indif-

21. *Congressional Record,* July 25, 1956, p. 14458.

ferent" Republicans more united than theirs. Housing bills, like farm bills, were enacted through the workings of a Democratic-centered coalition. To the votes of almost all city Democrats were added the votes of a good majority of non-city Democrats and a sizable proportion of city Republicans. Five key postwar housing roll calls which demonstrate this voting pattern most vividly are presented here in Table 16.

TABLE 16. Votes of city and noncity congressmen of each party on six selected city roll calls, 1947–1962

Year	Issue	Votes			
		Dem. city cong'men	Dem. noncity cong'men	Rep. city cong'men	Rep. noncity cong'men
1949	Passage of Housing Act of 1949	92–9	104–47	18–16	17–119
1949	Passage of Rent Control Act of 1949	96–5	108–48	23–9	38–97
1951	Second Conference Report of Independent Offices Appropriation bill: vote on Republican motion to insist on limiting construction of public housing units to 5,000 rather than 50,000 units	10–77	38–94	19–21	118–32
1954	Vote on Democratic motion to recommit Eisenhower omnibus housing bill and add authorization for construction of 140,000 public housing units over a 4-year period	70–12	71–55	20–32	33–129
1959	Passage of second omnibus housing bill	101–3	143–29	16–19	42–73

(On each motion, the ayes are given first, the nays second.)

Congressman Spence needed only to survey the voting records of his fellow Democrats to find refutation of his assertion. Northern rural congressmen supported the party position almost reflexively. In the Southern delegation of about a hundred congressmen, party leaders were able to count on the support of a minimum of about thirty-five, most of them from districts predominantly rural, for party housing policies. There were always at least thirty-two Southern votes for subsidized public housing, and the omnibus housing programs offered by Democrats after the 1958 election were favored by a majority of Southerners. Just as there were city Democrats who backed farm programs while proudly claiming that their districts had no farms, there were Southern rural congressmen who endorsed city housing programs while proclaiming that their districts had no urban slums.

And yet it is undeniable that the Democratic party was more successful in attracting the support of its "indifferent" congressmen for farm programs than for housing programs. City opposition to agricultural subsidies was minimal, but most Southerners usually chose to play the game of intraparty reciprocity only when on the receiving end. Opposition to costly urban programs was doubtless greater in Southern constituencies than opposition to the more inscrutable farm programs was in the Northern cities. Moreover, federal farm programs served the dominant economic interests in the South; programs designed to aid lower income city dwellers evoked entirely different political passions.

The size of party majorities in Congress was of critical importance in these years. The defection of about sixty Southerners from party ranks was enough to defeat Democratic proposals for strong federal rent control standards in the late 1940's, and to cripple the public housing program in the early

1950's. In an important sense, however, the balance of power was held by Northern voters. Because of the monolithic unity of Northern Democratic congressmen, party gains or losses in Northern districts — whether in Idaho, Kansas, or New York — usually meant gains or losses in votes for city housing programs. Accordingly, the most sweeping programs were passed by the House after the impressive Democratic congressional victories in 1948, in 1958, and in 1960. But fluctuations in the political fortunes of congressmen and housing bills should not conceal the fact that coalition patterns in housing matters were constant in both parties. In each party there were the loyal and the disloyal. But, on these questions of concern to city dwellers, dissent in the Democratic party came from those who claimed to "know very little about New York" and cared less; dissent in the Republican party came from the heart of the city.

4/THE PARTIES AND THE WORKER

"There appears to be a conspiracy to unionize the whole Nation."
— CONGRESSMAN LEO E. ALLEN OF ILLINOIS, RANKING REPUBLICAN ON HOUSE RULES COMMITTEE[1]

THE 1947–1962 PERIOD can quite plausibly be treated as a unit in the field of labor legislation. After the passage of the Wagner Act and the Fair Labor Standards Act in the 1930's, the postwar tone was set in 1947 by the enactment of the Taft-Hartley Act — either, according to the viewpoint of the pleader, a needed redress of management grievances or a body blow struck at the working man. The Eighty-first Congress disproved very soon the notion that Taft-Hartley could be repealed, and subsequent Congresses confined their attentions to marginal revision of the act in one direction or the other. Taft-Hartley became rather quickly a comfortable issue, with congressmen's positions a matter of historic record. After 1949, belaboring of the act was seldom inspired by expectations of radical change.

The enactment of minimum wage legislation — once a controversial undertaking — became in the postwar years a cherished congressional routine. The principle of federal wage and hour standards having been established in 1938, postwar disputes revolved around narrower questions of coverage and the level of the wage floor. By periodically raising the statutory minimum wage to match increases in living costs, Congress was able to generate an image of accomplishment.

1. *Congressional Record,* April 24, 1952, p. 4382.

The years after 1947 were, in short, fairly placid ones in the field of labor legislation; in Congresses under Truman, Eisenhower, and Kennedy, the balance of power precluded further drastic innovation. Only in the late 1950's and early 1960's did Congress turn to new kinds of programs affecting labor — area redevelopment and manpower retraining — programs offered as a response to the new problem of a secular rise in unemployment.

All this is not to say that postwar labor enactments were of no consequence. Unions learned to live with the Taft-Hartley Act because it did not, contrary to their predictions, seriously impair their bargaining power in organized industries. The act probably was, however, a significant deterrent to the enrollment of unorganized workers in unions.[2] The 1959 Landrum-Griffin Reporting and Disclosure Act placed new burdens upon unions and may have further inhibited organizational efforts.[3] Even minimum wage revision, often little better than a ritual, had some substance to it in 1961 when coverage was extended to 3,600,000 previously excluded workers. And although Congress, in 1962, had not yet evidenced a willingness to mount a general attack on the problem of persistent unemployment, the depressed areas and manpower training programs were experimental first steps.

LABOR ISSUES AND LABOR DISTRICTS

The subject under scrutiny here is the role of party in the treatment of labor legislation in the House. In the 1947–1962

2. See Joseph Shister, "The Impact of the Taft-Hartley Act on Union Strength and Collective Bargaining," *Industrial and Labor Relations Review*, 11:339–351 (April 1958).

3. See Philip Taft, "The Impact of Landrum-Griffin on Union Government," *Annals of the American Academy of Political and Social Science*, 333:130–140 (January 1961), and Edward B. Shils, "The Impact of Landrum-Griffin on the Small Employer," *Annals of the American Academy of Political and Social Science*, 333:141–152 (January 1961).

period, both parties consistently elected congressmen from working-class districts. If the assumption holds that congressmen representing workers are disposed to be sympathetic toward labor interests, then each party in the House must have faced the problem of taking into account the wishes of a minority of "labor congressmen." A clue to the solution arrived at by each party may be found in the relations which prevailed — in voting on labor issues — between its congressmen from labor and from nonlabor districts. In view of the public images of the two parties, a finding that Democrats and Republicans differed in their approaches to labor questions would not come as a shock.

In these years there were fifty-six House roll call votes that can safely be called "labor votes." Included are votes dealing with wages, unemployment, union powers and activities, and the operations of executive agencies with statutory duties in the labor field. Most attention was devoted to minimum wage (nine roll calls); area development, or "depressed areas," programs (nine roll calls — Majority Leader John McCormack and Rules Chairman Howard Smith led the House through eight consecutive procedural roll call votes before settling down to consider area redevelopment in 1960; only the last of these procedural votes is counted here); passage and 1949 reconsideration of the Taft-Hartley Act (seven roll calls); unemployment compensation (five roll calls); and the reporting and disclosure legislation of 1958–1959, including the Landrum-Griffin bill (five roll calls). Attempts to slice appropriations for various activities of the Labor Department produced a series of eight votes in the spring of 1957.[4] The fifty-six roll calls

4. The rest of the roll calls were on regulation of welfare and pension funds (three votes); amendment of the Railway Labor Act in 1950–51 (three votes); Administration handling of the 1952 steel strike (three votes); passage of the Portal-to-Portal Pay Act in 1947 (one vote); amendment of the Employers' Liability Act in 1947 (one vote); reorganization of the

were not uniformly distributed over the eight congressional sessions; only seven votes were recorded in the 1951–1956 period of conservative control. Moreover, the clusters of votes for the different sessions are not as usefully comparable as those on either farm or housing legislation; the voting alignments, for instance, on the Taft-Hartley Act in 1947 differ somewhat from those on area redevelopment in 1961. For some purposes, however, voting averages will be presented for each Congress, the seven votes for the 1951–1956 period being considered as one cluster.

The methodology used here requires the identification of a number of "labor districts" and "labor congressmen." Congressional districts whose blue collar workers comprised, in 1950, 55 percent or more of their total employed persons have been arbitrarily designated as "labor districts," and their Representatives therefore as "labor congressmen." [5] There were 128 such districts both before and after the wave of redistricting in the early 1950's. In the Eighty-third Congress (1953–1954), when new district lines had just been drawn, there were 18 "labor districts" in the old Confederate states, 8 in the Mountain and Pacific states, 33 in the Midwestern and Plains states (including here Kentucky and Oklahoma), and 69 in the New England and Middle Atlantic states (including West

National Labor Relations Board in 1961 (one vote); and passage of the Manpower Development and Training Act in 1961 (one vote).

5. The district blue collar percentages were taken from *Congressional Quarterly Weekly Report,* July 20, 1956. The figures are based on 1950 census data; blue collar workers include craftsmen, foremen, machine operators, private household help, service employees, and all other laborers except farm workers. Since *Congressional Quarterly's* statistics cover only post-1952 districts, there is again the problem of dealing with boundary changes just after the census. Blue collar percentages for discontinued pre-1952 whole-county districts have been calculated directly from the 1950 census data. Whether to include discontinued intracounty districts as labor districts has been decided by extrapolating from the later blue collar percentages in roughly the same geographical areas.

Virginia). Pennsylvania, with 23, had more than twice as many as any other state. Only about half the districts were predominantly urban. The Republicans held a maximum of 68 labor seats in 1947–1948, and a minimum of 35 in 1949–1950.

Labor districts have been isolated in the foregoing manner because it is assumed that the size of district blue collar labor force constitutes a useful measure of constituency influence on congressmen; Representatives from heavily blue collar districts presumably had cogent reasons for being pro-labor. In actuality, whether a congressman had to be attentive to labor desires depended upon much more than the number of workers he represented. A congressman who served a mining district in West Virginia or an auto district in Detroit — a district dominated by one union — was likely to find the signal from home to be loud and clear. For a congressman from a district with diverse unions, some of them all but apolitical, the signal was considerably more faint. A congressman whose workers were unorganized may have received no signal at all. In particular, it should not be thought that Northern and Southern congressmen with blue collar forces of equal size experienced similar constituency pressures, for Southern workers were less likely than their Northern counterparts to be either voters or union members. Figures showing the organizing success unions had enjoyed by 1953 in selected Northern and Southern states are given in Table 17. In short, the blue collar index is a useful, but by no means a definitive, indicator of constituency demands on labor matters.

In the studies of agriculture and housing, it was assumed that congressmen respectively from nonfarm and noncity districts not impelled by constituency pressures to be especially fervent in opposing the programs of their farm and city colleagues. To a great extent, the argument was between the farmer or city dweller and the unorganized taxpayer. Labor's

TABLE 17. Union membership in selected Northern and Southern states, 1953

State	No. of congressional districts in state with blue collar workers comprising 55.0 percent or more of total employed persons	Blue collar workers as a percentage of total employed persons in state	Organized workers as a percentage of total nonagricultural wage and salary workers in state
Pennsylvania	23	59.4	39.9
Ohio	11	55.0	38.0
Massachusetts	10	56.1	30.1
New York	10	50.7	34.4
New Jersey	9	54.8	35.2
North Carolina	4	49.3	8.3
South Carolina	3	49.7	9.3
Virginia	3	50.7	17.4
Georgia	2	49.8	15.0
Tennessee	2	47.1	22.6

Source: Blue collar percentages were taken from U.S. Bureau of the Census, *U.S. Census of Population: 1950*, II, Characteristics of the Population. Unionization percentages were taken from Leo Troy, *Distribution of Union Membership among the States: 1939 and 1953*, Occasional Paper 56 (New York: National Bureau of Economic Research, Inc., 1957).

argument very often was with management, and few constituencies permitted their congressmen to be indifferent bystanders; congressmen not answerable to labor were likely to be answerable to management. The use here of the blue collar index rests on the supposition that congressmen from districts where workers did not dominate the electorate tended to find merit in the positions of management.

That the articulation between working class electoral strength and congressmen's votes was not a perfect one may be shown in a presentation of cohesion indices for all labor and all nonlabor congressmen (party lines disregarded) on labor roll call votes. Mean cohesion indices for the different congressional sessions are given in Table 18. The typically low

TABLE 18. Mean cohesion of labor and nonlabor congressmen on labor roll calls in postwar Congresses

	Congressional sessions					
	1947–1948	1949–1950	1951–1956	1957–1958	1959–1960	1961–1962
All labor	22	56	36	29	45	54
All nonlabor	64	34	58	25	31	24
Number of roll call votes	(7)	(8)	(7)	(12)	(10)	(12)

cohesion of both blocs suggests the possibility that party ties intervened to override expected constituency ties. The hypothesis of party influence is reinforced by an examination of the disparities among the figures in the Table. The sharp reversal of cohesion levels in 1949–1950 is directly attributable to the fact that, in both labor and nonlabor districts, a good number of Republicans were replaced by Democrats in the 1948 election.

PARTY PRESSURES

In the coverage of postwar farm and city legislation, it was argued that the parties were exceedingly important in shaping congressional actions, that in each field opposing party pressures produced coalition voting patterns that recurred whenever Congress considered controversial farm or housing issues. In each field, Democrats consistently mobilized impressive proportions of their "indifferent" congressmen to forward the legislative aims of most Democrats and many Republicans from "interested" districts. Whether similar durable alignments existed on labor questions will be tested in the following analysis. Consideration will be given to the relationship between "labor" and "nonlabor" wings of each party in postwar votes on labor matters. Evidence of party operations will be sought in an examination of cohesion indices for the two wings of each party and of the voting records of elected leaders in each party.

The use of cohesion figures rests, once again, on the assumption that a wing of a party subjected to coinciding party and constituency pressures will demonstrate high cohesion, and that a party wing subjected to conflicting pressures will normally demonstrate low cohesion. In Figure 14, frequency distributions of cohesion indices are presented for labor and nonlabor congressmen of each party on the fifty-six labor votes. Republican nonlabor congressmen were clearly more united than their Democratic counterparts, Democratic labor congressmen more united than their Republican counterparts. The most irregular of the four groups was the labor Republicans, whose frequency distribution turns out to be bimodal. Republicans from labor districts were divided on area redevelopment and the 1957 Labor Department budget cuts, but were fairly solid — and loyal to the party — on questions of labor-management relations; the disparity in behavior will be given further attention. With suitable discount allowed for this Republican eccentricity, the differing cohesion patterns do suggest strongly that the Democrats espoused labor policies popular with their labor members and sought support for them in their nonlabor wing. The indication is that the Republicans embraced policies favored by their nonlabor wing and tried to gain backing for them among their labor congressmen.

An additional clue to party operations may be gained by focusing on the votes of elected party leaders. On those roll

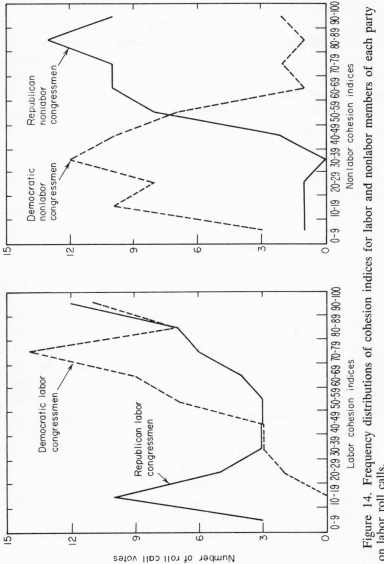

Figure 14. Frequency distributions of cohesion indices for labor and nonlabor members of each party on labor roll calls.

calls where the labor and nonlabor wings of a party were in significant disagreement, to which side did the leaders of the party normally lend their prestige and their votes? Democratic labor and nonlabor congressmen differed significantly on fifty-two of the fifty-six roll calls, Republican congressmen on only twenty-eight. The twenty-eight roll calls which divided Republicans include eight of nine on area redevelopment and all eight on the 1957 budget cuts, but only four of nine on minimum wage and three of twelve on the Taft-Hartley and Landrum-Griffin legislation. The set of figures below, an indication of the proclivities of party spokesmen on the divisive issues, shows respectively how many times the leaders of each party sided with their labor members, were divided themselves, and sided with their nonlabor members.

| Republicans | 4 | 2 | 22 |
| Democrats | 44 | 7 | 1 |

The pattern is clear. Democratic leaders sought consistently to rally their party behind members from labor districts. Republican leaders quite often maintained harmony within the party, but, when forced to make a choice, they came down in favor of the nonlabor position.

The unity of the Democratic leaders, usually one urban Northerner and one rural Southerner, on labor questions was extraordinary. Only eight other Southerners could be found to aid in upholding President Truman's veto of the Taft-Hartley bill, but Sam Rayburn's position was unambiguous: "I cannot support this bill and I am not going to." [6] The only roll call on which both Democratic leaders voted with the nonlabor wing of the party was a 1959 vote approving the conference report of the Landrum-Griffin bill. (It should be added that the prevailing party outlook was not always shared by the

6. *Congressional Record*, April 17, 1947, p. 3665.

Chairman of the important Education and Labor Committee. In the 1950's the Committee, though stocked with liberal Democrats, was led by Graham Barden of North Carolina. Barden thought as little of labor unions as he did of New York City, and his retirement in 1960 must be cited as a variable in any explanation of why minimum wage legislation could be passed in 1961 but not in the previous year.)

On the Republican side, the party leaders probably experienced their most trying days under President Eisenhower. Their normal course was to reinforce the position of the non-labor wing of the party, now and then voting with the labor members on passage of watered-down bills, namely, the minimum wage bills of 1955 and 1961 and the manpower retraining bill of 1962. Under Eisenhower, this habitual mode of operation produced intermittent conflict with the Administration. House leaders could not agree with Secretary of Labor James Mitchell on minimum wage policy. The Administration favored some kind of depressed areas legislation, but House Republican spokesmen twice supported moves to prevent floor consideration of the depressed area problem. In 1957, Mitchell's departmental budget was defended by Democrats and by a heavy proportion of labor Republicans against the assaults of the House Republican leadership.

The cohesion data and the records of party leaders point to a conclusion that labor controversies evoked essentially the same kind of coalition voting alignments that appeared on farm and housing issues. The Democratic party bolstered the positions of congressmen from "interested" districts and the Republican party pulled in the other direction. Democratic defections occurred among nonlabor members, Republican defections among members from blue collar districts. In succeeding pages, the workings of each party will be examined more closely.

THE REPUBLICANS

The legislative activities of Republicans from labor districts must be approached with some caution. When party loyalty scores are calculated for each Republican labor district in the sixteen-year period, the resultant frequency distribution in Figure 15 reveals a good many districts with low scores. (As in the previous analyses, each loyalty score here is based on the voting records of all congressmen of a party serving a single postwar district if they served it in at least three Congresses of the eight.) But Republican labor members behaved differently on different issues. The mean index of likeness for labor and nonlabor Republicans on the twelve Taft-Hartley and Landrum-Griffin votes is 95; the voting records of labor members on these two measures were not substantially different from those of other Republicans. The mean likeness index on the nine minimum wage votes is a high 89, but on the nine area redevelopment votes a low 72. All the fifty-six postwar labor votes were on matters of material consequence to workingmen, but Republican congressmen serving working-class districts exhibited a greater willingness on some issues than on others to vote in defiance of party policies.

Questions of labor-management relations inspired Republicans to their greatest unity. It should be pointed out that, in 1947, the Hartley bill passed by the House was considerably more unacceptable to the unions than the final Taft-Hartley bill reworked in conference; the House bill, for example, would have abolished industry-wide bargaining. (The content of the conference version was geared to the requirement of winning a two-thirds vote in the Senate to override an anticipated Presidential veto; House approval was taken for granted.) Yet opposition to the Hartley bill offered by House Republicans from labor districts is hardly worthy of mention; it differed in

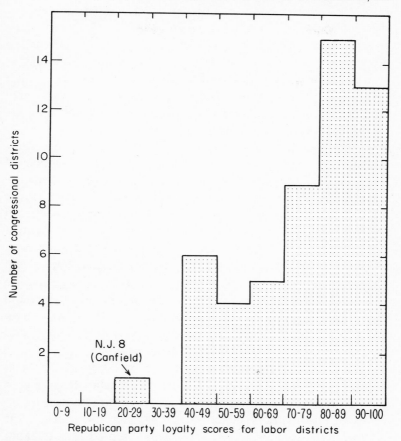

Figure 15. Frequency distribution of party loyalty scores for Republican labor districts.

orders of magnitude from the clamor raised by Farm Belt Republicans in the same Congress when the party leadership sought to undermine New Deal farm programs. Of some sixty-five labor Republicans, only thirteen broke with the party at any stage of consideration of the Hartley and Taft-Hartley bills. Nor did the 1948 election produce conversions on the issue. Twenty-three Republicans from labor areas who voted with the leadership in 1947 and who survived the election were given an opportunity to recant in 1949; only one — Congressman John Bennett of the Michigan Upper Peninsula — voted for repeal of Taft-Hartley. A decade later, the record of party fidelity on the Landrum-Griffin reporting and disclosure legislation was about the same.

Republican leaders also maintained a high level of party harmony on minimum wage legislation, probably because of their habitual support of a modicum of upward revision. The most severe intraparty strain occurred in 1955, when House leaders sought enactment of a ninety-cent minimum wage bill after the Senate had already voted for a dollar. Carroll Kearns, Representative of a Pennsylvania labor district and a power on the Education and Labor Committee, asked Republican leader Halleck to explain "why the House should be put on the spot for 90 cents?" [7] The dollar wage won on a teller vote, and the indications are that there were heavy defections among labor Republicans. Over the years, however, most labor members found party wage policies to be congenial.

When compared with their behavior on labor-management relations and minimum wage, the actions of labor Republicans on area redevelopment legislation can be characterized as explosive. The districts which stood to gain most under the depressed areas programs are generally counted here as labor districts, a good many of them — especially in Pennsylvania — served by Republican congressmen. A bill was finally passed in 1961, after the depressed areas issue had plagued the Republican party during the two preceding congressional sessions and two election campaigns. President Eisenhower had put forth modest proposals in the field, but vetoed more ambitious

7. *Congressional Record,* July 19, 1955, p. 10947.

Democratic bills in 1958 and 1960. House Republican Whip Leslie Arends dismissed the whole effort as "a vast socialistic scheme." [8] Unable to follow the party line, Republicans from labor surplus areas dissented vigorously in House debate; majorities of Pennsylvania labor Republicans voted with the Democrats on all nine roll calls on the issue. James Van Zandt of Pennsylvania, critical of the official party position, recalled in 1961 his recent campaign experiences: ". . . [F]rankly I apologized to the many unemployed residents of my district for the vetoes, and especially the one of last year." [9]

If it is accepted that the issues discussed above — labor-management relations, minimum wage, and area redevelopment — are issues in which labor spokesmen were vitally interested, there arises the problem of explaining the differential reactions of Republican labor congressmen. More labor Republicans deserted their party on area redevelopment than on the other matters. The first thing to be said is that the attitudes of working-class constituents on labor-management questions are by no means clear and overwhelming. The difficulty of interesting union members in the Taft-Hartley Act has been recorded.[10] And, besides being relatively inscrutable to the layman, the postwar labor-management bills shared with minimum wage bills the attribute of affecting most deeply the fortunes of workers outside of labor unions and often outside of major labor areas. It is quite possible that area redevelopment was a more pressing issue in the Pennsylvania Republican constituencies than either minimum wage proposals or reforms in labor-management relations.

But surely the most convincing explanation of the differences in Republican behavior is a more obvious one. In breaking

8. *Congressional Record,* August 15, 1958, p. 17848.
9. *Congressional Record,* March 29, 1961, p. 5249.
10. V. O. Key, Jr., *Public Opinion and American Democracy* (New York, 1961), pp. 509–511.

party ranks to protect the Labor Department budget in 1957, or to support Democratic depressed area bills, Republicans from labor districts could be prolabor without really being antimanagement. The area redevelopment program, like the farm and housing programs, was essentially a federal subsidy to a particular section of the country; it provoked the conventional argument in Congress between "spenders" and "savers." Legislation dealing with the wage structure or with the rights of unions and management, however, went to the heart of the employer-employee relationship. Issues which stirred passions of equal intensity in unions and in management could be expected to produce congressional reactions rather different from those produced by issues in which management was not vitally interested.

In addition, the evidence suggests that the concern of House Republican leaders about postwar labor issues varied directly with the concern of management. The Republicans seem to have moved heaven and earth to put across the Landrum-Griffin amendment in 1959. In the words of one of Charles Clapp's anonymous Democratic congressmen, "On the labor issue Republicans were exerting all sorts of pressure. Administration leaders came down and cajoled Republican congressmen to go along with them. Post Office patronage was certainly held out to these members. They control the purse strings. If a man goes along, he gets money for his campaign; if he doesn't go along he gets nothing. It's that simple." [11] Two of Clapp's Republicans agreed that there was pressure: "While we cannot deny that there was a lot of pressure put on in the labor bill, that was a party vote calling for teamwork. I believe in teamwork." [12] "Pressure on the labor bill was somewhat justified since I think it was the key vote in the

11. Quoted in Clapp, *The Congressman*, p. 319.
12. Clapp, p. 315.

Congress." [13] The fidelity of labor Republicans on postwar labor-management questions is probably traceable in some degree to the fact that the party whip was applied on these questions with special energy. Manufacturers accustomed to filling party coffers doubtless expected due consideration when their fortunes were directly at stake.

The impression should not be given, however, that area redevelopment was the only issue to lure Republicans away from party moorings; the attractiveness of opposition on that issue was just much greater than on most others. Some Republicans voted with the Democrats more often than not on labor issues, and the figures suggest that size of district blue collar population was a relevant variable for congressmen considering the advisability of party loyalty. The mean party loyalty score for seventeen Republican districts with blue collar percentages in the 55.0 to 57.4 range was 81, the average score for twenty-four districts in the 57.5 to 59.9 range an almost identical 80. In twelve Republican districts, however, blue collar workers comprised more than 60.0 percent of the employed population, and the mean loyalty score of their servants was a considerably lower 63.

Included in the heavily blue collar category were the districts listed in Table 19. Some of the loyalty scores recorded in the Table are high. That of Louis E. Graham (Pennsylvania 25) is inexplicably high. Joe Martin, Speaker in the Eightieth Congress, even suggested that Graham vote *against* the Taft-Hartley legislation. "We've got plenty of votes," Martin told him. "If I were you, I'd think it over. You've got a bad district." [14] Graham insisted on voting for Taft-Hartley, and for all other Republican labor policies; his district turned Demo-

13. Clapp, p. 315.
14. Joe Martin, *My First Fifty Years in Politics* (New York, 1960), p. 183.

TABLE 19. Party loyalty records, on labor issues, of Republican congressmen from heavily blue collar districts, 1947–1962

District	Congressmen	Blue collar percentage	No. of recorded votes of all district cong'men	Party loyalty score for all cong'men serving each district
Pa. 12	Fenton	69.4	54	63
Pa. 26, 22	Tibbott, Saylor	66.2	51	41
Pa. 25	Graham	64.1	21	100
W.Va. 1	Love, Moore	63.2	41	49
Pa. 22, 20	Van Zandt	62.0	56	57
N.J. 8	Canfield	61.8	38	29
Conn. 5	Patterson	61.8	29	41
Mass. 14	Martin	61.8	42	81
Mass. 9	Gifford, Nicholson, Keith	61.7	54	85
N.H. 1	Merrow	61.4	52	65
Pa. 19, 23	Gavin	60.4	56	70
Me. 2	Smith, Nelson, Tupper	60.2	32	72

cratic in 1954 and remained safely Democratic thereafter. Joe Martin, himself from a labor district, embraced party labor positions while he was Republican leader, but began to vote with the Democrats more often after being deposed in 1959; his cumulative score is a fairly high 81. Most of the loyalty scores listed in Table 19, however, are rather low, and the likelihood is that Republicans with more than 59 or 60 percent of their constituents blue collar workers had to entertain serious doubts about the wisdom of party policies. In the 1960 election, Republicans were able to elect Congressmen in only nine districts out of fifty-two with 60 percent blue collar populations; consistent party success in a respectable share of districts of this type probably would have reduced party cohesion in the House.

THE DEMOCRATS

A case can be made that labor issues have divided the Democratic party by section more clearly and consistently than any other issue except race. Laws regulating wages and union operations have affected North and South differently and can easily be viewed as sectional legislation. Democrats dominant in the Southern social hierarchy have tended to frown upon unions and all their works; Northern labor leaders and their Democratic spokesmen have viewed the thralldom of Southern workers as a threat to the political and economic security of Northern labor. The result has been intraparty controversy, and Democratic congressional leaders from the South — such as Sam Rayburn and Hale Boggs — have usually had trouble finding very many Southern colleagues who would support party labor policies.

Among non-Southern Democrats from all kinds of districts, however — at least in the 1947–1962 period — a prolabor attitude prevailed. The figures in Table 20 suggest the closeness of ties between Northern Democrats from labor and nonlabor districts. (In Table 20 and in the following tables and figures the South, unless otherwise indicated, will again be taken to include only the eleven Confederate states, the North the remaining states.) The lowest mean cohesion indices are for the 1947–1948 and the 1959–1960 congressional sessions, a reflection of the fact that about a third of nonlabor Northerners — many of them from border states — sided with the Republicans on the Taft-Hartley and Landrum-Griffin bills. These

TABLE 20. Solidarity of Northern Democrats on labor issues

	Congressional sessions					
	1947–1948	1949–1950	1951–1956	1957–1958	1959–1960	1961–1962
Mean cohesion of all Northern Democratic congressmen	55	97	84	84	78	94
Mean likeness indices for Northern labor and Northern nonlabor Democratic congressmen	66	99	88	94	89	97

serious delinquencies aside, harmony was the rule. All but three non-Southerners joined in the party effort to repeal the Taft-Hartley Act in 1949, and Northern resistance on minimum wage bills was negligible. All told, on thirty-six of the fifty-six labor roll calls fewer than ten Northerners voted against the dominant party position. On occasion there was opposition to the party line from within the ranks of labor. Erratic behavior by congressmen from mining districts in Pennsylvania, West Virginia, Ohio, and Kentucky was a signal that the United Mine Workers and the Democratic leadership were at odds. The miners opposed a "mild" reporting and disclosure bill (the predecessor of Landrum-Griffin) put forth by the Democrats in 1958, and a bill regulating union welfare and pension funds in 1962.

That Northern labor was the tail that wagged the dog in the House Democratic party is suggested by the persistently high loyalty scores registered by Northern labor members; the distribution of scores is given in Figure 16. Democratic enshrinement of prolabor programs as party policies ordinarily made the prolabor position the majority position in the party. The

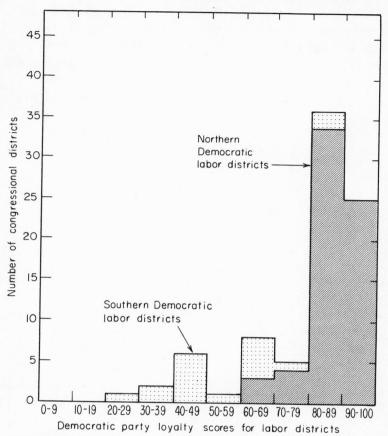

Figure 16. Frequency distribution of party loyalty scores for Democratic labor districts.

modal district loyalty score in Figure 16 is in the 80's; it would be up in the 90's had the votes of the Eightieth Congress been excluded. The subjugation of Northern Democrats in the 1946 election temporarily placed both Northern laborites and the party leadership in the minority in House Democratic ranks.

The apostasy of Southern Democrats on labor issues can be demonstrated more easily than it can be explained. Taken as a group, the Southern delegation found Republican labor policies in these years much more attractive than Democratic

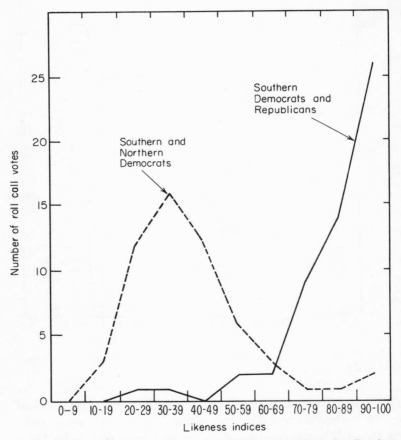

Figure 17. Frequency distributions of likeness indices for Southern and Northern Democrats and for Southern Democrats and Republicans on 56 postwar labor roll calls.

policies. As shown in Figure 17, there is a striking difference between the likeness indices for Southern and Northern Democrats and for Southerners and Republicans. But here the difficulty begins, for Southern aversion to party notions on labor was neither an all-encompassing nor a random phenomenon. A good number of Southerners demonstrated a steady willingness to go along with the party. The disparity in party loyalty among Southern districts is shown in Figure 18. The problem is to account for the differences among Southerners.

Any analysis of the predispositions of Southern congressmen is complicated by the fact that throughout this postwar era they still represented truncated electorates; demographic characteristics of Southern districts were less automatically reflected in congressional sentiment than those of Northern districts. Hence it is not astonishing that use of the blue collar index unearths no abiding differences among Southern congressmen of the period on labor matters. The wide spectrum of party loyalties among the Southern labor members may be observed in Figure 18; the propensity of labor members to divide like other Southerners on labor questions is indicated in the high mean likeness indices for labor and nonlabor congressmen in the period:

1947–1948	1949–1950	1951–1956
90	94	89

1957–1958	1959–1960	1961–1962
94	86	81

Southerners from labor areas typically found distinctive merit in the official party position only on the final passage of minimum wage bills—but not on critical preceding amendments.

There were some labor districts — for instance, the Second Texas district in the Beaumont-Port Arthur area — where

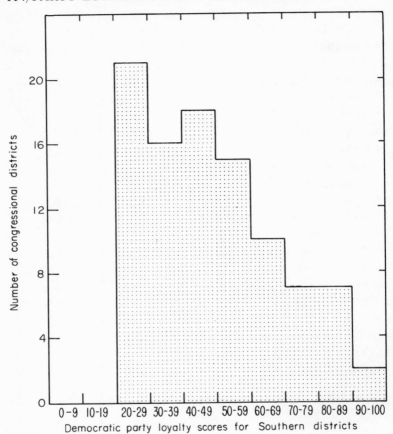

Figure 18. Frequency distribution of party loyalty scores for Southern Democratic districts on postwar labor issues. As in the previous city analysis, a loyalty score is included here for a Southern district if it elected Democrats to at least five postwar Congresses.

unions had to be reckoned with, but congressmen from the Southeastern textile belt lived in a simpler world. The saga of the Seventh Georgia district is instructive. The district was in the industrial northwestern section of Georgia, and, had it been in the North, its 59.1 blue collar percentage would almost certainly have assured in its congressmen a due solicitude for the working man. The constituency was served for many years by Henderson Lanham, who was strongly prolabor, but who harbored no illusions about the political necessity of being so: "There are union organizations in only 4 of my 14 counties. Moreover, we have the county-unit system in Georgia, so that the labor organizations in these four counties are not able to elect one Representative." [15] Lanham's successor was another liberal, Erwin Mitchell, who served one full term and then retired from Congress in 1960 with a blast at "the sham and hypocrisy that permeates the ranks of the Democratic Party in the South." [16] Richard Bolling reports that Mitchell left Congress to regain his health; he was leveled by the "round-the-clock harassment" of business lobbyists during the Landrum-Griffin struggle of 1959.[17] In 1960 the district sent to Washington a more conservative Democrat.

In the previous city analysis, in an effort to find demographic correlates of Southern congressional behavior on housing issues, figures showing percentage Negro population in each Southern congressional district were introduced.[18] The expectation was that the traditional Southern cleavage between Black Belt conservatism and highland liberalism would be reflected in the roll call voting of postwar Southern congressmen. A test of the hypothesis here on labor issues yields worthwhile results. Party loyalty in Southern districts (except, once again,

15. *Congressional Record,* April 29, 1949, p. 5337.
16. Address before the Seventh District Democratic Executive Committee at Rome, Georgia, quoted in *Congressional Record,* May 12, 1960, pp. 10225–10226.
17. Bolling, *House Out of Order,* p. 168.
18. The Negro percentages were taken from *Congressional Quarterly Weekly Report,* March 30, 1962. The *Congressional Quarterly* figures are actually for "nonwhite" population, but can be read as "Negro" population in considering Southern districts.

those in Texas, where the traditional cleavage has not existed) on labor issues tended to vary inversely with percentage Negro population; the figures are in Table 21. At least it may be said

TABLE 21. Relation between party loyalty of Southern Democratic congressmen on labor issues and district Negro percentages, 1947–1962

	Percentage Negro population in districts				
	0.0–9.9	10.0–19.9	20.0–29.9	30.0–39.9	40.0 and over
Mean district loyalty scores	63	58	39	46	36
Number of districts	(8)	(13)	(24)	(22)	(11)

that districts with fewer than 20 percent Negroes were more likely than those with over 20 percent to send party regulars to Congress.

A closer examination of the data discloses that there were markedly different patterns in different Southern states. Figures for selected states are presented in Table 22. In Alabama, Tennessee, and Arkansas, the negative relationship between Negro population and labor loyalty is very striking. On the other hand, in North Carolina, where the conflict between coastal and Piedmont areas has been atypical by Southern standards, no clear pattern emerges. Undifferentiated conservatism prevailed in most of Virginia and Mississippi. Table 22 suggests the importance of relations within state delegations in determining voting positions.[19] It should be noted that some delegations seem to have been more loyal as a whole than

19. See David B. Truman, "The State Delegations and the Structure of Party Voting in the U.S. House of Representatives," *American Political Science Review*, 50:1023–1045 (December 1956).

TABLE 22. Southern Democratic loyalty on labor issues as a function of Negro percentage, in selected states, 1947–1962

District	Cong'men	Negro percentage	Party loyalty
	ALABAMA		
7	Manasco, Elliott	9.9	91
5	Rains	15.8	88
8	Jones	16.0	89
4	Hobbs, Roberts	31.7	76
9	Battle, Huddleston	34.6	67
2	Grant	36.0	41
6	Jarman, deGraffenreid, Selden	38.7	53
1	Boykin	38.8	56
3	Andrews	39.3	36
	ARKANSAS		
3	Trimble	2.3	88
2	Mills	12.0	63
5	Hays, Alford	18.6	53
7, 4	Harris	29.5	53
6	Norrell, Mrs. Norrell	30.0	46
1	Gathings	32.5	28
	VIRGINIA		
9	Flannagan, Fugate, Jennings	2.7	73
7	Harrison	8.2	28
5	Stanley, Tuck	23.2	22
8	Smith	24.4	23
3	Gary	25.8	30
2	Hardy	28.3	43
1	Bland, Robeson, Downing	29.1	24
4	Drewry, Abbitt	48.0	30

District	Cong'men	Negro percentage	Party loyalty
	MISSISSIPPI		
6	Colmer	23.8	21
4, 1	Abernethy	32.2	23
5	Winstead	41.2	21
7, 4	Williams	46.4	24
2	Whitten	49.6	24
3	Whittington, Smith	65.5	44
	TENNESSEE		
5, 4	Evins	7.0	71
7, 6	Courtney, Sutton, Bass	13.0	88
3	Kefauver, Frazier	13.3	70
6, 5	Priest, Loser	19.2	57
8, 7	Murray	25.2	25
9, 8	Cooper, Everett	26.3	52
10, 9	Davis	36.4	51
	NORTH CAROLINA		
12	Redden, Shuford, Hall, Taylor	7.6	50
9	Doughton, Alexander	12.5	38
11	Bulwinkle, Jones, Whitener	13.0	40
8	Deane, Kitchin	22.4	47
6	Durham, Kornegay	23.1	47
5	Folger, Chatham, Scott	24.3	23
4	Cooley	27.8	60
3	Barden, Henderson	29.6	32
7	Clark, Carlyle, Lennon	35.6	35
1	Bonner	43.8	38
2	Kerr, Fountain	50.5	49

others; congressmen from heavily Negro areas of Tennessee and Alabama were by and large more loyal than congressmen from equivalent areas in Virginia and Mississippi.

Another way to confront the problem of Southern differences in loyalty is to hypothesize that Democratic presidential voting strength in the South was by 1960 a rough measure of liberal sentiment. (There were, to be sure, religious distortions in 1960, but there were other distortions in the Eisenhower

TABLE 23. Relation between party loyalty of Southern Democratic congressmen on labor issues, 1947–1962, and district Kennedy percentages, 1960

	Percentage of total district vote cast for Kennedy			
	Under 40.0	40.0–49.9	50.0–59.9	60.0 and over
Mean district loyalty scores	35	43	56	49
Number of districts	(12)	(25)	(36)	(24)

elections.) In the figures in Table 23, a relationship is drawn between loyalty of Southern districts — Texas districts included — on labor issues and the Kennedy percentage of the total presidential vote in 1960.[20] The correlation is, up to a point, an impressive one, indicating that there was a tendency for conservative constituencies to sustain conservative Democrats in Congress but to bolt the party in presidential elections.

Further light can be thrown on the loyalty problem by cross-tabulating the figures for Negro population and Kennedy strength. The result is Figure 19, which measures the relationship between labor loyalty and Democratic presidential strength in districts with low, medium, and high proportions of Negroes in the population. The data, though thin in places, are suggestive. In Southern districts least convulsed by the race problem, the tendency was strong for voters to demonstrate ideological consistency in choosing congressmen and President; consistency declined as Negro percentage rose. However, in districts competitive on the presidential level (40.0 to 59.9 percent Democratic), labor loyalty varied directly with Democratic presidential percentage at all levels of Negro population.

20. Voting percentages were taken from *Congressional Quarterly Almanac,* 87th Congress, 1st Sess., 1961, pp. 1033–1075.

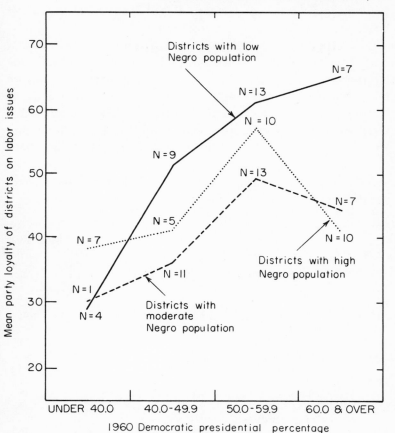

Figure 19. Party loyalty of Southern Democratic congressmen on labor issues as a function of district Negro percentage and district Kennedy percentage in 1960. Figures are included for districts that elected Democrats to at least five postwar Congresses.

The most interesting pattern appears in the safe Democratic districts, where congressmen with moderate to heavy Negro populations scored low in party loyalty. A good number of these safe districts were Black Belt constituencies in states —

Georgia, for instance — where Republicanism had not yet become fashionable among conservatives.

The general conclusion to be drawn from Figure 19 is that party loyalty on labor issues was by no means random among Southerners. As in the North, clues to a district's outlook on labor policy could be sought in its social structure and in its partisan preferences. Southern districts whose congressmen were most friendly to labor are listed in Table 24, along with some district characteristics. (Some of the Texas and Southern

TABLE 24. Southern districts whose Democratic congressmen scored highest in party loyalty on labor issues, 1947–1962

District	Congressmen	Blue collar per- centage	Negro per- centage	Democratic presidential percentage, 1960	Party loyalty on labor issues
Tex. 1	Patman	42.1	26.7	57.9	92
Ala. 7	Manasco, Elliott	35.4	9.9	54.8	91
Ala. 8	Jones	38.5	16.0	68.8	89
La. 6	Morrison	48.5	35.4	50.6	89
Ala. 5	Rains	50.0	15.8	65.0	88
Ark. 3	Trimble	36.3	2.3	40.7	88
Tenn. 7, 6	Courtney, Sutton, Bass	39.4	13.0	63.7	88
La. 2	Boggs	56.1	31.0	53.3	85
Tex. 2	Combs, Brooks	59.0	31.6	58.8	85
Ala. 4	Hobbs, Roberts	53.3	31.7	57.7	76
Va. 9	Flannagan, Fugate, Jennings	55.9	2.7	51.0	73
Tex. 3	Beckworth, Gentry, Beckworth	47.8	24.7	46.5	72
Tenn. 5, 4	Evins	37.3	7.0	55.7	71
Fla. 4	Smathers, Lantaff, Fascell	50.4	14.6	58.0	70
Tenn. 3	Kefauver, Frazier	55.7	13.3	42.1	70
Tex. 8	Thomas	53.6	26.1	56.5	70

Louisiana districts had sizable Negro populations and also sustained liberal congressmen. One reason for this is that Negroes were allowed to vote in these areas.)[21] By and large, the predispositions of Southern congressmen on labor questions matched their predispositions on housing questions; in Figure 20 a comparison of district party loyalty scores for the two kinds of issues shows the strength of the relationship.

The importance of party ties is demonstrated in the consistency with which a number of Southern congressmen, apparently unimpelled by constituency pressures, supported Democratic labor policies designed to please organized labor. Most Southerners in Congress were antilabor, but the weight of Democratic party influence tended to unite the North and divide the South — thereby enrolling sizable majorities for the prolabor position.

This examination of a diverse collection of fifty-six postwar labor votes discloses a coalition pattern essentially similar to those in agriculture and housing. Conflicting party pressures superimposed on conflicting constituency pressures produced unity among labor Democrats and nonlabor Republicans, disunity among nonlabor Democrats and labor Republicans. The Democrats, as in farm and housing matters, rallied party support for programs favored by congressmen of both parties from "interested" districts. Democrats from labor areas rivaled farm and city Democrats in inviting intraparty reciprocity. Congressman Lanham of Georgia, in supporting the 1955 minimum wage revision, gave voice to the characteristic party philosophy and the spirit of logrolling which sustained it: "So far as I have been able I have tried to approach all legislation

21. See John H. Fenton and Kenneth N. Vines, "Negro Registration in Louisiana," *American Political Science Review,* 51:704–713 (September 1957), and Harry Halloway, "The Negro and the Vote: The Case of Texas," *Journal of Politics,* 23:526–556 (August 1961).

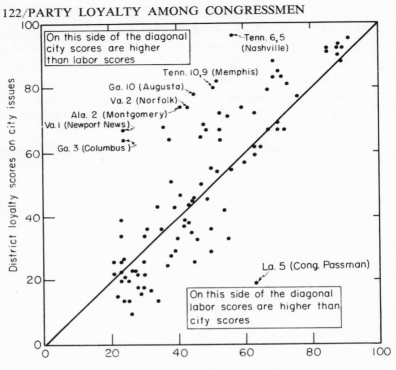

Figure 20. Relation between party loyalty of Southern Democratic congressmen on labor issues and loyalty on city issues, 1947–1962. Each dot represents a congressional district.

on the basis of what is good for the entire country. I voted the other day for the development of a reclamation project in California, and I am going to vote for one on the Northern Colorado pretty soon." [22]

On votes involving appropriations or federal subsidies, the Democratic-centered labor coalition tended to function smoothly. In direct confrontations with management, erosion

22. *Congressional Record,* July 20, 1955, pp. 11084–11085.

of strength at the margins of the coalition — among Southerners and labor Republicans — produced a rather consistent record of failure. A sample of postwar voting is presented in Table 25. Thirteen roll call votes, selected for their importance, are ranked according to a descending order of Republican

TABLE 25. Votes of labor and nonlabor congressmen of each party on selected postwar labor roll calls

Year	Issue	Votes of Rep. nonlabor cong'men	Votes of Rep. labor cong'men	Votes of Dem. nonlabor cong'men	Votes of Dem. labor cong'men	Rep. intraparty likeness indices	Dem. intraparty likeness indices
1947	Overriding of Taft–Hartley veto	168–8	60–3	93–34	14–39	100	53
1949	Attachment of crippling Lucas Amendment to minimum wage bill	117–11	32–3	70–97	13–77	100	72
1949	Attachment of antilabor Wood Amendment to bill repealing Taft–Hartley Act	116–17	30–5	61–105	12–77	99	76
1961	Disapproval of Kennedy reorganization of N.L.R.B.	123–8	38–5	70–104	13–73	94	75
1947	Passage of Hartley bill	162–14	55–10	82–42	13–44	93	57
1960	Attachment of crippling Kitchin Amendment to minimum wage bill	97–18	27–9	80–103	13–78	91	70
1959	Adoption of Landrum–Griffin Amendment	104–10	30–7	82–107	13–78	90	71
1961	Attachment of crippling Ayres Amendment to minimum wage bill	113–16	32–10	67–104	9–76	88	72
1962	Vote on Ashbrook Amendment (to welfare and pensions bill) restricting AFL–CIO organization of Labor Department employees	101–26	26–16	52–111	9–71	82	79
1952	Vote on Smith resolution advising use of Taft–Hartley injunction to stop steel strike	118–27	28–20	73–60	13–62	77	62
1960	Motion to recommit area redevelopment bill	102–13	23–12	49–130	4–83	77	78
1957	Motion to cut funds for unemployment compensation	129–21	29–20	54–99	12–63	73	81
1958	Motion to recommit area redevelopment bill	112–30	23–24	48–93	11–64	70	81

intraparty likeness indices. It will be seen that, on different issues, there was a tendency for higher levels of defection among labor Republicans to be accompanied by higher levels of intraparty harmony among Democrats. The attitudes of labor Democrats and nonlabor Republicans were close to unshakable; which side was victorious on an issue depended primarily upon the decisions of labor Republicans and nonlabor Democrats — upon the decisions of congressmen who often found party and constituency pressures incompatible.

The assertion was made earlier that a historical account of congressional treatment of labor legislation in the 1947–1962 period possesses a certain unity. The unvarnished truth is that unions — when strongly opposed by management — were handed by the House an embarrassingly unbroken string of defeats. With Northern Democrats reduced to a core in the Eightieth Congress, the passage of the Taft-Hartley Act did not come as a total surprise. But in no subsequent Congress did labor have the upper hand. In the heavily Democratic Eighty-first Congress, the House buried Taft-Hartley repeal and emasculated a minimum wage bill on the floor. The attitude of the Democratic Eighty-second Congress toward the 1952 steel strike was resonantly hostile. Nor did the sweeping Democratic victories in the 1958 and 1960 elections produce any significant change in labor fortunes. House members elected in 1958 — 283 of them Democrats — rushed to Washington to pass the Landrum-Griffin Act; crippling amendments were attached to minimum wage bills in both 1960 and 1961. Area redevelopment aside, postwar Congresses did perilously little in the labor field without official Republican approval.

5/THE PARTIES AND THE WEST

"The good Lord put this Colorado River on the west side of the Rocky Mountains. The advocates of this bill now wish to dig a hole through the mountains and put part of it over on the east side of the mountains. I think if it was intended to be over on the east side of the mountain the good Lord would have put it over there himself."
— CONGRESSMAN HOWARD SMITH OF VIRGINIA, CHAIRMAN OF HOUSE RULES COMMITTEE[1]

THE WEST occupies a special place in American history and folklore. The pioneering spirit that wrested the Mountain and Pacific states from the Indians and from the elements finds even now an echo in the cult of rugged individualism prevalent in the large Southwestern cities. The paradox is that, in fact, economic self-sufficiency has been much less possible for individuals in the West than it was in the areas settled earlier in the East and Midwest. Civilization in much of the West is artificial and fragile, a product of cooperative effort and federal subsidy. Los Angeles is an invention, not a discovery.

The critical variable is water. Nature provides the West with ample water but so little of it at the right times in the right places that most of the area is naturally desert wasteland. As a result, dams, ditches, and aqueducts have to be constructed to satisfy the water requirements of both farmer and city-dweller. All this costs money, and the source of much of the capital for the harnessing of the great Western rivers in this

1. *Congressional Record*, July 26, 1956, p. 14801.

century has been the federal government. The Colorado, the Columbia, and the Rio Grande have been tamed with federal help, and the waters of the California Central Valley have been redistributed to match local needs. The most recent federal undertaking of magnitude has been a program to dam the Upper Colorado and parcel out its waters for irrigation purposes.

The concern with water gives a peculiar cast to Western politics. Congressional elections are said to turn on the success or failure of incumbents in producing dams for their constituents. A perennial conflict rages between California and the other states along the Colorado over the disposal of the waters of that river. In addition, the economics of dam construction renders the issue of public power inseparable from that of irrigation and reclamation. At times, as in the Hells Canyon controversy of the 1950's, entire river basins seem to be agitated over the question of who shall build what dams and what attendant transmission lines.

Western Republicans point with pride to the fact that it was President Theodore Roosevelt who stimulated Congress to pass the 1902 Reclamation Act. Eastern Republicans, however, have looked upon reclamation — with its costs and its public power consequences — as warily as they looked upon Theodore Roosevelt. In the 1930's, the Administration of Franklin Roosevelt undertook ambitious projects on the Columbia and in the Central Valley and, in general, brought a new fervor to federal reclamation policy. In the years after World War II the Democrats, if they could lay a claim to being the party of labor, the party of the city, and the party of the farmer, could also lay a claim to being the party of reclamation. The recent achievement of the Democrats in destroying traditional Republican hegemony in California and Oregon can doubtless be traced in some measure to popular assessment of the parties' differing water policies.

WESTERN ISSUES AND WESTERN DISTRICTS

Both Democrats and Republicans consistently harbored sizable delegations of congressmen from the Western states in the 1947–1962 period. How did each party deal with its Westerners? Once again, the assumption is that some clue to party operations can be found in the relationship that prevailed — on selected roll call votes — between members of a party from "interested" districts and those from relatively "indifferent" districts. Here each party was confronted by the constituency needs of congressmen whose people enjoyed a special and historic connection with the federal government.

Issues of peculiarly Western impact do not submit to precise delineation. For this chapter, ninety-two postwar roll call votes on matters presumed to have been of uncommon concern to Westerners have been isolated. Thirty-one of the votes dealt with federal reclamation activities in general, with specific Western reclamation projects, or with the activities of Western power authorities established to handle electric power generated at federal dams. Fourteen of the votes were on rivers and harbors authorizations or public works appropriations. The Army Engineers served the whole nation, but the West derived special benefits from their efforts. The included public works appropriations supplied funds for both the Army and the Bureau of Reclamation. Fifteen of the votes were on federal atomic energy programs. The question of what to do with atomic energy developed in the 1950's into a contest between public and private power interests, with special attention being devoted to the problem of whether to build atomic reactors with federal funds in the Pacific Northwest.

Thirteen of the votes dealt with Alaskan and Hawaiian state-hood. The supposition is that Westerners were more eager than most other Americans to add two new Western states to the Union. Twelve of the votes were on federal programs sub-sidizing the production of lead, zinc, and other minerals — a particular concern of the Mountain states.[2] It will be seen that most of the ninety-two roll calls dealt with water and public power, but that a substantial number reflected other Western concerns.

The methodology employed here requires an identification of a specific block of congressional districts with specific issues of moment in those districts. The districts taken to be Western here are all those in the eight Mountain states (Arizona, Colorado, Idaho, Montana, Nevada, New Mexico, Utah, and Wyoming), in the three Pacific states (California, Oregon, and Washington), and, after extension of statehood, in Hawaii and Alaska. This definition of "the West" is an arbitrary one. The states traditionally served by the Bureau of Reclamation include also the tier of six Plains states ex-tending South from North Dakota to Texas. A drawing of the East-West boundary just east of the Rockies, however, eliminates the political currents of the Farm Belt and the South and narrows the focus to those areas in which the physical environment has been particularly hostile. Roll calls dealing in general terms with reclamation and public power are as-sumed here to have been of concern to the West, but roll calls on specific reclamation projects and power authorities are considered only if the interests of any of the enumerated

2. The remaining seven votes were on federal timberlands policy (1954); a proposed transfer of functions from the Interior to the Agriculture Department (1959); the water rights of farmers along the Santa Margarita River in California (1952); establishment of a national historic site in Arizona (1960) and a national tropical botanical garden in Hawaii (1960); settlement of a land claim in the Grand Canyon (1962); and authorization of expenditures in Mount Rainier National Park (1960).

Western states were specifically at stake. It should be noted that the included Western districts — numbering forty-nine in 1947 but fifty-nine by 1962 — varied considerably in their characteristics. Some congressmen watched over the interests of thousands of square miles of wasteland in Wyoming and Nevada; others served concentrated populations in downtown Los Angeles. Almost all Western congressmen, however, could be stirred by mention of the water problem.

It is reasonable to expect that Western congressmen should have enlisted rather frequently in bipartisan moves to forward the interests of their section. And indeed they did. The comparative cohesion indices in Table 26 indicate that Western

TABLE 26. Mean cohesion of Western and non-Western congressmen on Western roll calls in postwar Congresses

	Congressional sessions							
	1947–1948	1949–1950	1951–1952	1953–1954	1955–1956	1957–1958	1959–1960	1961–1962
All Western	51	84	34	45	56	37	46	42
All non-Western	23	16	15	13	24	12	33	15
Number of roll call votes	(7)	(7)	(10)	(9)	(13)	(17)	(12)	(17)

congressmen were consistently more united than their non-Western colleagues in voting on Western issues. Westerners approached unanimity in the Eighty-first Congress, the post-1948 Congress in which Republican leaders — perhaps suffering from shock induced by the election — seem to have refrained from forging and enforcing opposition policies on many kinds of issues. This relative solidarity of the Western delegation contrasts sharply with the extremely low cohesion of Easterners. The West being in the minority, its welfare depended heavily upon the political machinations of non-Western congressmen; the explanation for abiding divisions among Easterners on Western issues must be sought in the operations of the two parties.

PARTY PRESSURES

The short answer to the question of how the parties responded to the needs of their Western Congressmen is that the Democratic party was measurably more hospitable than the Republican to Western interests. The tendency was for Democrats to accord Western programs such as reclamation projects and mineral subsidies the same generous reception they reserved for housing projects and farm subsidies. The tendency was for Republicans to look upon all with a jaundiced eye. The difference in the approaches of the two parties can be demonstrated in the cohesion displayed by segments of each and in the records of party leaders.

In Figure 21, frequency distributions of cohesion indices, calculated from votes recorded on the ninety-two Western roll calls, are presented for the Western and non-Western elements of each party. There emerges a striking disparity between the voting behavior of Western Democrats and that of Western Republicans. Solidarity was the norm among Democratic Westerners, but their Republican colleagues were usually divided. Among non-Western congressmen, however, Republicans surpassed Democrats in achieving party harmony on Western issues. These cohesion patterns suggest strongly that Democratic party strength was customarily marshaled to reinforce the legislative stands of Western members, and that Republican party strength was more often used to reinforce Eastern resistance to Western demands.

The difference in party attitudes on Western matters ap-

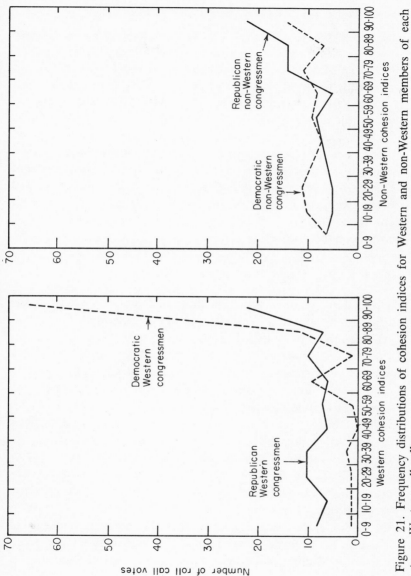

Figure 21. Frequency distributions of cohesion indices for Western and non-Western members of each party on Western roll calls.

pears clearly in the votes of elected party leaders (Floor Leaders and Whips). When the Western and non-Western segments of a party were significantly divided in their voting, with which side did the leaders of the party customarily align themselves? Eastern and Western Republicans differed significantly on fifty-nine of the ninety-two roll calls, Eastern and Western Democrats on fifty-two. The data given below indicate that, when intraparty divisions occurred, Republican leaders normally reinforced the stands of their Eastern members and Democratic leaders voted with the West; the figures record respectively the number of times that the leaders of each party embraced the Western position, were divided themselves, and embraced the non-Western position.

Republicans	14	5	40
Democrats	46	2	4

These data, in brief, buttress the conclusion drawn from the cohesion figures that Western Democrats benefited, and Western Republicans suffered, from the flow of party pressures.

It was the custom for House Democratic leaders to confer blanket endorsement of Western reclamation, public power, or minerals programs about which there was controversy. In Democratic ideology, the West was a just claimant to federal favors. "When the roll call comes," said John McCormack in deploring Republican cuts in the Interior budget in the Eightieth Congress, "the people of the great West and Northwest will see on that roll call that the majority of the Democratic members will be where they have always been on these propositions — and that is, in support of these appropriations for these great progressive projects." [3] Eastern backing of Western programs was construed as a self-denying act. Congressman Michael Kirwan of Ohio, the generous guardian of

3. *Congressional Record,* April 25, 1947, p. 4045.

Interior Department interests on the House Appropriations Committee, characteristically remarked in defending the 1951 Interior appropriation, "I can assure you that there is not $40,000 in this bill for the State of Ohio, and not a quarter for my district." [4] Democratic leaders seemed to desert their Western delegation only when more important federal policies were at stake — as in their refusal to allow concessions to mining interests in the amending of the Defense Production Act in 1951, or when Westerners themselves were in disagreement — as in the leaders' opposition to the Fryingpan-Arkansas Project in 1954.

The Republican House leadership, like the Democratic, had to face the harsh realities of Western politics. In the Eisenhower years, Republican leaders compiled a rather impressive record in advocacy of specific reclamation projects requested by Republican congressmen and endorsed by the Administration. Party strength was summoned in support of the Rogue River Project (Oregon) in 1954, the Little Wood River Project (Idaho) in 1956, the Fryingpan-Arkansas Project (Colorado) in 1954 and 1956, and the ambitious Upper Colorado Storage Project in 1956. In addition, House leaders backed a 1958 Administration measure designed to subsidize lead and zinc mining. Republican control of the White House seems to have had a moderating effect upon the opposition psychology of the party on the Hill.

All this, however, went against the grain. Charles Halleck stated his position in 1952: "I recognize, as do many of us, the strong political attraction that is alleged to stem from the fact that you vote money for this particular project or that particular project, hoping thereby to curry the favor of the particular people who want that appropriation made, but may I point out to my friend [McCormack] that in the broader

4. *Congressional Record,* April 23, 1951, p. 4193.

concept in this country there is an overwhelming demand that the expenses of the Federal Government be reduced. That demand is the direct result of a growing conviction in the country on the part of all right-thinking people that we are rapidly spending ourselves into bankruptcy and ruin." [5] Significantly, official Republican support for the Western position was often less visible on the more inscrutable appropriations bills than it was on authorizations; party leaders led assaults on Interior Department budgets in 1947 and 1951 over the objections of their own Western members. There was, in addition, a distinctive Republican antipathy reserved for programs which contributed to the expansion of public power. All told, in the roll calls of the sixteen years on which Eastern and Western Republicans divided, party leaders voted with their Western members only fourteen times out of fifty-nine. And five of these fourteen votes were on Hawaiian statehood, a project for which Republican spokesmen — proceeding under the interesting assumption that Hawaii would turn out to be a Republican state — long exhibited a special fondness. (Democrats, of course, evinced a comparable solicitude for Alaskan longings, and for like reasons.)

THE REPUBLICANS

It would be a gross mistake to say that Westerners have been unanimous in their views on regional projects. Examples of wrangling among resident interests are legion. Arthur Maass has documented the Byzantine intricacies of the Kings River controversy, in which the warring Army Engineers and Reclamation Bureau both had their California adherents.[6] In

---

5. *Congressional Record,* March 26, 1952, p. 2972.
6. *Muddy Waters: The Army Engineers and the Nation's Rivers* (Cambridge, Mass., 1951), chap. v.

struggles over public power expansion, private electric companies have regularly found support among many Western Republicans. In Utah, in 1962, a disagreement over whether to create a sizable new national park in the canyonlands of southeastern Utah easily became a partisan disagreement, with Republicans upholding the position of mining companies.[7]

Nevertheless, the fact remains that, in the West, the rain fails to fall on Democrats and Republicans alike. Postwar congressmen of both parties had to champion reclamation projects, and, in some states, men of both parties chose to favor mineral subsidies or public power programs. No congressman lacked constituents highly conscious of the West's dependence upon the federal government. Weighty problems were thereby created for Western Republican congressmen, who often had to choose between the claims of their electorates and the austere outlook of their party.

A lesson in what could happen when Republicans possessed a strong working majority in Congress was provided for Western Republicans in the operations of the Eightieth Congress. Party leaders, in control of the relevant Appropriations subcommittee, struck out at New Deal reclamation policies in the same way they attacked New Deal farm policies; the Truman Administration's Interior Department budget was cut in half. Western Republicans, some of them impeccably conservative, surveyed with anguish the expected impact upon projects in their home states. Congressman Wesley D'Ewart of Montana was "deeply concerned."[8] Congressman Bertrand Gearhart of California, a protector of the Central Valley Project, argued that "the Congress, in this stubborn indifference to realities, is rendering a decided disservice, not only

7. *New York Times,* February 4, 1962, and October 4, 1962.
8. *Congressional Record,* April 24, 1947, p. 3982.

to the far West but to the entire country." [9] Congressman
Norris Poulson of Los Angeles christened the appropriation
measure the "discrimination against the West" bill.[10] All in all,
thirteen Republican congressmen from eight Western states
rose in the House to protest the party's action. Out West, ten
governors held a bipartisan conference and assailed the cuts.[11]
The uproar resulted in the restoration of some of the funds
in the Senate and in conference.

Columbia Valley Republicans who expressed a regional de-
sire for public power expansion enjoyed a particularly hostile
reception in party councils. In 1947, 1951, and 1953, there
were floor contests over funds for the Bonneville Power Administration, with Republicans from Oregon and Washington
joining in the opposition to their party's appropriations policy.
Congressman Homer Angell of Portland termed the handling
of Bonneville funds by the Eightieth Congress "an outrage to
our state." [12] Between 1956 and 1962 a controversy raged
over federal construction of an atomic reactor for generation
of electric power at the Hanford plutonium plant in Washington. Again Northwestern Republicans, isolated in their own
party, turned to the Democrats for support of their power
program. John Kessel writes that, in 1962, Washington congressmen of both parties worked as a unit in pressing their
pleas.[13]

The positions adopted by Eastern Republicans and party
leaders on Western issues induced most Westerners to defect
frequently from party ranks. Some of them voted more than

9. *Congressional Record,* April 25, 1947, p. 4104.
10. *Congressional Record,* April 25, 1947, p. 4087.
11. *Congressional Quarterly Almanac,* 80th Congress, 1st Sess., 1947,
p. 196.
12. *Congressional Record,* July 26, 1947, p. 10462.
13. John H. Kessel, "The Washington Congressional Delegation," *Midwest Journal of Political Science,* 8:1–21 (February 1964).

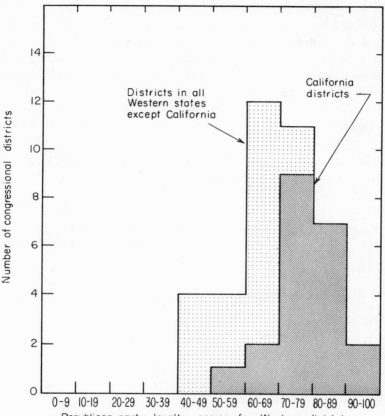

Figure 22. Frequency distribution of party loyalty scores for Republican Western districts.

half the time with the Democrats. In Figure 22, a frequency distribution of party loyalty scores for Western Republican districts on Western issues, the modal party loyalty score is in the 60's. (Each loyalty score is, again, based on the votes of all congressmen of a party serving a single postwar district if they served it in at least three Congresses of the eight.) Congressmen from urban California, serving districts less immediately involved in water, public power, and minerals problems, found party regularity slightly more attractive than those serving outlying areas. Republican districts with the lowest loyalty scores are listed in Table 27.

Disloyalty was most common in Washington and Oregon — a reflection of the importance in these states of the public

TABLE 27. Western districts whose Republican congressmen ranked lowest in party loyalty on Western issues, 1947–1962

District	Congressmen	No. of recorded votes of all district cong'men	Party loyalty score for all cong'men serving each district
Wash. 5	Horan	90	40
Ore. 3	Angell	27	41
Wash. 4	Holmes, May	91	45
Wash. 6·	Tollefson	82	46
Colo. 3	Chenoweth	83	53
Ore. 2	Stockman, Coon	44	57
Wash. 2	Westland	65	58
Cal. 6	Baldwin	59	58
Ore. 1	Norblad	83	60
Colo. 2	Hill, Dominick	73	60
Wyo. AL	Barrett, Harrison, Thomson, Harrison	83	63
Ariz. 1	Rhodes	64	64
Cal. 3, 11	Johnson	45	64
Wash. 1	Jones, Pelly	72	65
Utah 2	Dawson	46	67
Cal. 4	Mailliard	58	67
Ore. 4	Ellsworth, Durno	56	68
Wash. 3	Mack	67	69
Utah 1	Stringfellow, Dixon	51	69
Mont. 2	D'Ewart, Fjare, Battin	61	69

power issue — but districts with low loyalty scores were liberally sprinkled throughout most of the Mountain states. "Since I have been a Member of this Congress," Congressman John Rhodes, an Arizona Republican representing a traditionally Democratic district, lamented in 1955, "I have noticed with increasing alarm that many of the Representatives from the States east of the Mississippi have felt that reclamation was some sort of a boondoggle which was meant only for the western part of the United States." [14] Unhappily, the source of the Congressman's alarm was to be found in the attitudes not of Eastern congressmen in general but of Eastern Republicans.

THE DEMOCRATS

Democrats boast that theirs is the only truly "national" party, and their record in dealing with the West adds some strength to the claim. In the postwar years House Democratic majorities were summoned with regularity in support of Western reclamation, public power, and mineral subsidies. The party loyalty scores of Western Democrats, shown in Figure 23, stand in clear contrast to those of Western Republicans. Democrats from all Western districts found the party position on home issues a tenable one more than 80 percent of the time.

These loyalty figures are, of course, more a measure of Eastern than of Western attitudes. In Western matters, as in farm, housing, and labor matters, Northern Democrats provided the reservoir of support that made party fealty in "interested" districts possible. The close relationship that prevailed between Western and other non-Confederate Democrats

14. *Congressional Record,* May 26, 1955, p. 7140.

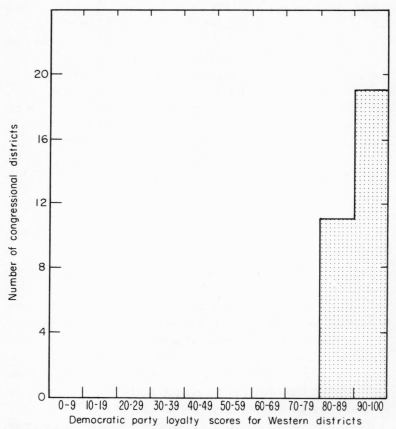

Figure 23. Frequency distribution of party loyalty scores for Democratic Western districts.

is indicated in the high mean likeness indices for the two groups in voting on Western issues in the postwar Congresses.

1947–48	1949–50	1951–52	1953–54
89	79	82	85

1955–56	1957–58	1959–60	1961–62
89	87	93	85

Northeastern Democrats offered sustained opposition to only one major Western program: federal construction of atomic reactors. Democrats from Pennsylvania and other coal-producing states joined Republicans in viewing development of atomic power as a threat to their already declining home industry.

Southern Democratic congressmen, in voting on Western concerns, followed their customary course of giving less complete support to party policies than Northerners. The Southern position on Western issues, however, unlike the regional position on labor matters, was closer to the sentiments of Northern Democrats than to those of Republicans. The frequency distribution of likeness indices in Figure 24 demonstrates this Southern preference. (The South is defined again as the Confederacy.) The fact that the South, like the West, has benefited from federal water projects doubtless facilitated Southern support of Western programs. Southern congressmen from constituencies served by the Tennessee Valley Authority and the Southwestern Power Administration regularly displayed a sympathy for public power expansion in the West.

The roll call voting reveals, however, the existence of no special coalition devised by Southerners and Westerners to serve their mutual interests. Southern support for Western programs flowed through the well-worn channels of the Democratic coalition. The data in Figure 25 show the relationship between Southern party loyalty on labor issues and loyalty on Western issues. Of the ten Southern districts whose congressmen scored lowest in party loyalty on Western issues, three — Mississippi 6 (Colmer); Virginia 5 (Stanley, Tuck); and Virginia 8 (Smith) — were in the lowest ten on labor issues. Of the ten Southern districts most loyal on Western issues,

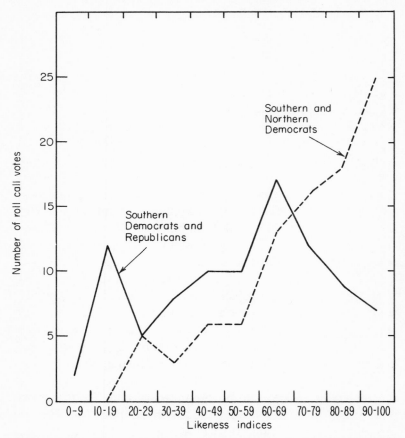

Figure 24. Frequency distributions of likeness indices for Southern Democrats and Republicans and for Southern and Northern Democrats on 92 postwar Western roll calls.

five — Alabama 8 (Jones); Arkansas 3 (Trimble); Louisiana 6 (Morrison); Tennessee 7, 6 (Courtney, Sutton, Bass); and Texas 2 (Combs, Brooks) — appear in a list of the ten districts most liberal on labor issues.

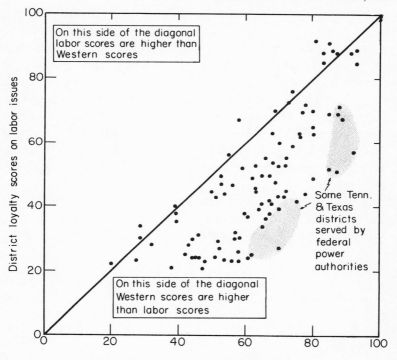

On this side of the diagonal labor scores are higher than Western scores

On this side of the diagonal Western scores are higher than labor scores

Some Tenn. & Texas districts served by federal power authorities

District loyalty scores on labor issues

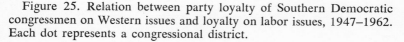

District loyalty scores on Western issues

Figure 25. Relation between party loyalty of Southern Democratic congressmen on Western issues and loyalty on labor issues, 1947–1962. Each dot represents a congressional district.

If congressmen dislike making hard decisions, postwar Democratic Westerners could take some joy in the fact that their party and constituency pressures usually coincided, that their party held in readiness an endorsement of their regional undertakings. With the support of almost all Northeastern Democrats and a sizable number of Southern Democrats and Western Republicans, the chances were good that a bill could be translated into an enactment.

The development of the natural resources of the West has been in many ways a bipartisan effort. Presidents of both parties have had dams named after them, and Western congressmen of both parties have often found it easy to agree on the needs of the region. The argument here has been, however, that the parties in the House in these sixteen postwar years responded to Western demands in fundamentally different ways. Controversial Western issues uncovered a recurrent House voting alignment, with Eastern Democrats supporting, and Eastern Republicans opposing the claims of their Western colleagues.

This difference in approach is demonstrated clearly in Table 28. In every Western state where comparisons are possible, Democratic congressmen were able to maintain much

TABLE 28. Proportions of votes, on 1947–1962 Western issues, cast by members of party delegations from each Western state in accordance with the positions of national party majorities

	Democrats			Republicans		
State	Total votes cast	Party loyalty on all 92 Western votes	Party loyalty on 31 reclamation and public power votes	Total votes cast	Party loyalty on all 92 Western votes	Party loyalty on 31 reclamation and public power votes
Alaska	29	97	100	0	—	—
Arizona	107	88	93	64	64	69
California[a]						
North	597	93	89	556	72	70
South	504	93	89	760	79	75
Colorado	191	87	87	163	56	48
Hawaii	22	100	100	0	—	—
Idaho	86	94	83	84	77	75
Montana	116	93	91	61	69	68
Nevada	61	97	100	27	74	56
New Mexico	168	87	89	0	—	—
Oregon	129	95	96	210	59	52
Utah	78	88	100	97	68	70
Washington	122	93	93	467	53	46
Wyoming	0	—	—	83	63	56

[a] California is divided in half, for purposes of demonstration; the dividing line, a traditional one, is the Tehachapi mountain chain just north of Los Angeles.

higher levels of party loyalty than Republicans in voting on postwar Western issues. The attitudes of Easterners were at the root of the disparity. The Western Republican, like the Western Democrat, had to look to the federal government for favors: "I plead with you and I urge you in the interest of national defense not to cut this appropriation for the Bonneville Power Administration." [15] The Eastern urban Democrat answered the call: ". . . I feel that the western section of our country is deserving of consideration and aid." [16] The reply of the Republican from the large Eastern state was more skeptical: "Where does the government get the money? The only place the government gets the money is from the American taxpayer and there are ten million of them in my state." [17]

15. Congressman Russell Mack (Wash. 3), *Congressional Record,* April 24, 1951, p. 4303.
16. Congressman Adolph Sabath (Ill. 7) on a mineral subsidy bill, *Congressional Record,* March 13, 1950, p. 3228.
17. Congressman Leon Gavin (Pa. 23) on the authorization of the Rogue River Project, *Congressional Record,* July 30, 1954, p. 12822.

6/CONCLUSION

"What about the Tennessee Valley Authority years ago and the dramatic fights that were waged in this House? . . . I spoke for the T. V. A. then. I spoke for Boulder Dam. I spoke for the first Bankhead Cotton Quota Act in 1933 . . . Other members from city or urban districts did the same. There was a solid urban vote in support of the Bankhead Cotton Quota Act, and on all subsequent legislation, because we are imbued with the spirit of Jefferson. We view our problems nationally and not from a sectional angle."

— CONGRESSMAN JOHN McCORMACK OF BOSTON,
DEMOCRATIC MAJORITY LEADER[1]

IT IS an important fact of American politics that a congressman dispatched to Washington to guard the interests of a district cannot do the guarding by himself. It takes the votes of as many as 218 congressmen to authorize the building of a dam, to pass a housing bill, to provide special economic assistance for "depressed areas," to extend aid to growers of Maryland tobacco or Kansas wheat, or to finance construction of a botanical garden in Hawaii. It is only natural, therefore, that there should develop among congressmen habitual channels of mutual accommodation. As one congressman has put it, "Unless special and sectional interests work out areas of accommodation with each other, there is no way for any of them to achieve their relatively narrow goals." [2]

1. *Congressional Record,* March 11, 1949, p. 2285.
2. Frank E. Smith, *Congressman from Mississippi* (New York, 1964), p. 139.

Nor is it surprising that mutual accommodation, or log-rolling, should be most common among members of the same political party. Wilfred Binkley, along with many others, has depicted the parties as instruments for welding together national coalitions of diverse interests.[3] Thomas Jefferson, in his botanical excursion of 1791, is said to have struck an alliance between New York politicians and Southern planters. Henry Clay's "American System" offered tariffs for the Northeast and internal improvements for the West. The Civil War Republicans appealed to Northern workers, businessmen, and farmers. William Jennings Bryan tied together South and West with a silver thread, and Franklin Roosevelt joined the clienteles of Bryan and Al Smith. In the years after World War II, the nation extended the usual hospitality to political parties and to special interests, and the former persisted in appealing to combinations of the latter.

COALITIONS AND COMPROMISE

In a perceptive discussion of the two parties, Dean Acheson has argued that "the principal clue in understanding the vitality and endurance of the Democratic party" is to be found in the "multiplicity of interests" it comprehends.[4] The party "performs through its own processes a preliminary accommodation and regulation of various and different interests before the legislative process begins, or as part of it, and by this develops policies and programs national in their scope and base."[5] On the other hand, Acheson goes on, "[t]he economic base and the principal interest of the Republican

3. *American Political Parties: Their Natural History,* 3rd ed. (New York, 1959).
4. Dean Acheson, *A Democrat Looks at His Party* (New York, 1955), p. 25.
5. Acheson, p. 32.

party is business," [6] and the governmental pursuits of Republicans reflect this single concern.

Whether these statements apply to the party struggles of the past may be questioned. Nevertheless, there is a ring of truth to them if one considers the parties of the years after World War II — specifically, the years 1947–1962. If Democrats and Republicans did differ in this fashion, how should the difference have been visible in congressional voting? Dankwart Rustow, in *The Politics of Compromise*,[7] has distinguished three patterns of legislative compromise. Assume the existence of a number of minority blocs each advocating its own programs. Where separate programs do not conflict, an "inclusive" compromise results in the acceptance of all of them. Where separate programs do conflict, an "exclusive" compromise results in the rejection of all programs not favored by any majority. Where financial differences occur, opposing blocs may "split the difference." Rustow symbolizes the three forms of compromise as follows (the arrows separate initial positions from resulting settlements).

$$a, b \rightarrow a + b \quad \text{(inclusive)}$$
$$a + b, b, b + c \rightarrow b \quad \text{(exclusive)}$$
$$a, b \rightarrow (a + b)/2 \quad \text{(split the difference)}$$

If the preceding studies of voting on farm, city, labor, and Western issues are compared, the most striking conclusion is that postwar Democrats and Republicans differed in precisely the same manner in their approaches to all these sets of domestic issues. That each congressional party handled Western and farm legislation in the same way it handled labor and housing legislation is a fact by no means obvious to the armchair

6. Acheson, p. 26.
7. *The Politics of Compromise: A Study of Parties and Cabinet Government in Sweden* (Princeton, N.J., 1955), pp. 230–232.

observer. In voting on each of the four sets of issues, however, Democrats from "interested" districts maintained higher cohesion than Democrats from "indifferent" districts. In the Republican party the reverse was true; members from "indifferent" districts demonstrated greater unity than members from "interested" districts. On all four kinds of issues, "interested" Democrats scored considerably higher in party loyalty than "interested" Republicans. House Democratic leaders persistently championed, and Republican leaders persistently opposed, the programs of their "interested" members. (A summary of leadership leanings on the four types of issues is presented in Table 29.) All this is to say that, on all four

TABLE 29. Leanings of party leaders on four kinds of domestic issues when their "interested" and "indifferent" wings were divided, 1947–1962

	Republicans		Democrats	
Issues	Leaders favoring positions of "interested" cong'men	Leaders favoring positions of "indifferent" cong'men	Leaders favoring positions of "interested" cong'men	Leaders favoring positions of "indifferent" cong'men
Farm	19	47	49	10
City	4	22	44	1
Labor	4	22	44	1
Western	14	40	46	4

issue sets, Republican and Democratic pressures flowed in the same opposite directions. Rustow's model of compromise offers relevant terminology for discussing the consistent difference in party approaches. (The "inclusive" and "exclusive" categories will be applied here. The "split the difference" form of compromise was frequently chosen when Senate and House disagreed on appropriations measures.)

It can be said that the Democratic party in these years was transcendently a party of "inclusive" compromise. The legislative demands of congressmen from the four kinds of districts examined here were not incompatible, for all these demands — with the exception of labor desires on labor-management questions — could be satisfied by various forms of federal aid. Some congressmen wanted dams, others wanted mineral subsidies, others wanted area redevelopment funds, others wanted housing projects, still others wanted farm subsidies. As a result, the House Democratic leadership could serve as an instrument for mobilizing support among all Democrats for the programs of Democrats with particular interests. "Indifferent" Democratic congressmen frequently backed such programs "even against the debatable best interests of the people of their own communities." [8] Republicans who characterized the Democratic party as a "gravy train" were quite right. John McCormack, not ordinarily known as a philosopher, expressed with great insight in his extemporaneous House speeches a philosophy of what the Democratic party was and what kept it bound together.[9] McCormack persistently argued that, on domestic economic questions, each segment of the party relied upon and deserved the support of all other segments of the party, and that a summation of the programs of the various party elements constituted the national interest. This Democratic outlook, as well as the pattern of legislative accommodation derived from it, was obviously fitting for a party wedded to an ideology of welfare liberalism. The essential point is that

8. Congressman Walter Lynch of New York, *Congressional Record,* March 15, 1948, p. 2876.

9. One of his best speeches on Democratic philosophy was delivered in support of federal rent control in 1949. *Congressional Record,* March 11, 1949, pp. 2284–2285.

the program of the Democratic party in the House — of party leaders and of party majorities — was arrived at by adding together the programs of different elements of the party. In Rustow's symbolism, the resulting "inclusive" compromise may be denoted as follows (with the demands of farm, city, labor, and Western congressmen assigned suitable initials).

$$F, \ C, \ L, \ W, \ \rightarrow \ F + C + L + W$$

This Democratic outlook, moreover, was not confined to Northerners. Because it was in agricultural matters that the South (that is, the Confederacy) was the principal beneficiary of party policy, no attempt was made in the farm study to analyze the attitudes of the few Southern "indifferent" congressmen on farm questions. On the three sets of issues of special concern to non-Southern Democrats, however, party loyalty scores were calculated for all Southern Democratic districts. The figures show that a sizable proportion of Southerners joined the nearly unanimous Northern wing in voting on city, labor, and Western issues. Southerners loyal or disloyal on one of the issue sets, moreover, tended to be equally loyal or disloyal on the others. (There were, of course, variations. Democrats from Tennessee and Texas gave heavier support to party policies on Western matters. A number of congressmen from districts with heavy Negro populations found party housing policies more palatable than party labor policies.) At the extremes, represented in Table 30, nine Southern districts elected congressmen who embraced party positions more than 80 percent of the time on city issues, on labor issues, and on Western issues; eight districts elected congressmen with cumulative party loyalty scores of lower than 40 on all three sets of issues.

The list in Table 30 displays the liberalism of northern Alabama and the conservatism of Virginia. It also suggests

TABLE 30. Southern districts whose Democratic congressmen scored consistently over 80 or under 40 in party loyalty on city, labor, and Western roll calls, 1947–1962

District	Congressmen	Party loyalty on city issues	Party loyalty on labor issues	Party loyalty on Western issues
Ala. 7	Manasco, Elliott	95	91	85
Ala. 5	Rains	92	88	83
Ala. 8	Jones	92	89	86
Ark. 3	Trimble	92	88	87
La. 2	Boggs	92	85	83
Tex. 1	Patman	92	92	81
Tex. 2	Combs, Brooks	91	85	83
Tenn. 7, 6	Courtney, Sutton, Bass	90	88	91
La. 6	Morrison	88	89	93
Tex. 7	Pickett, Dowdy	14	34	31
Va. 5	Stanley, Tuck	15	22	20
Va. 4	Drewry, Abbitt	18	30	29
Va. 7	Harrison	18	28	32
Va. 8	Smith	20	23	27
Miss. 6	Colmer	22	21	38
N.C. 9	Doughton, Alexander	28	38	39
N.C. 7	Clark, Carlyle, Lennon	36	35	39

something about the politics of the House Rules Committee — namely, that Rules in these years was not a haven for "moderates." In the Eighty-seventh Congress (1961–1962), its members included Carl Elliott (Alabama 7), James Trimble (Arkansas 3), Howard Smith (Virginia 8), and William Colmer (Mississippi 6) — all of them listed above as either loyalists or heretics. (The fifth Southern member was Homer Thornberry [Texas 10], whose district's postwar loyalty record on the three issue sets was a high 83–87–69.) In the "packing" of Rules in 1961, which involved the addition of a Republican, a Northern Democrat, and a Southern Democrat, the appointment of Elliott gave control of the Committee to Speaker Rayburn and the liberals.

Democratic supremacy in the South has long concealed, of course, a good deal of affection for Republican policy positions. It is reasonable to expect that postwar Southern constituencies which sustained conservative Democratic congressmen should have viewed Democratic presidential nominees with some alarm. The data in Table 31 show that a positive relationship

TABLE 31. Mean party loyalty scores of Democratic congressmen from Southern districts on three sets of issues, 1947–1962, as a function of 1960 Democratic presidential percentage

	1960 Democratic presidential percentages in districts			
	Under 40.0	40.0–49.9	50.0–59.9	60.0 and over
City issues	30	44	58	58
Labor issues	35	43	56	49
Western issues	55	57	69	68
Number of districts	(12)	(25)	(36)	(24)

existed in Southern districts between 1960 Democratic presidential percentage and party loyalty of congressmen on city, labor, and Western issues. Southern support was a critical element in Democratic legislative strategy on many kinds of postwar issues, but for a large number of Southern congressmen — serving, as did almost all Southerners, truncated electorates — disloyalty to party was a political necessity.

Acheson contends that the Republican party, unlike the Democratic, serves a single interest: business. The loyal Republican constituent is the taxpayer, William Graham Sumner's "forgotten man," the citizen who stands for free enterprise and economy in government. Attention has been given in the previous analyses to congressional districts "interested" in various federal programs. There were also, in these postwar years, a number of districts which did not fall into any of the four "interested" categories — they were sanctuaries, doubtless, of the "forgotten men" — and it should occasion no surprise that an impressive majority of them regularly elected Republican congressmen. A party breakdown of congressmen from the residual districts is given for each postwar Congress in Table 32. Although generalization about the character of

TABLE 32. Number of Republicans and Democrats serving districts not included in any of four "interested" categories, 1947–1962

Congress	Republicans	Northern Democrats	Southern Democrats	Total Democrats
80th	69	3	16	19
81st	60	11	16	27
82nd	64	7	16	23
83rd	68	7	17	24
84th	64	12	16	28
85th	66	10	16	26
86th	48	28	15	43
87th	56	20	15	35

these constituencies is hazardous, some statements can be made. There were a few in central Florida and in Texas, some in scattered suburban areas. By far the largest single grouping of them lay in the traditional Republican heartland — the belt of small towns and small cities, originally settled by New Englanders, stretching from upstate New York across Ohio and Michigan into northern Illinois. It was conservative Representatives from this area, men like John Taber and Daniel Reed of New York, Clarence Brown of Ohio, Leo Allen and Leslie Arends of Illinois, who long gave congressional Republicanism its distinctive tone.

And yet the Republican party, like the Democratic, harbored in the 1947–1962 period sizable numbers of congress-men from "interested" districts. A Clifford Hope of Kansas had to watch wheat prices, a John Saylor of Pennsylvania had to de-fer to labor, a John Lindsay of New York had to support hous-ing legislation, and a Walt Horan of Washington had to display some sympathy for public power. How did the party deal with its minorities? The Republicans, in Rustow's terms, were a party of "exclusive" compromise. *Whenever possible,* most Re-publican congressmen opposed federal spending programs and championed policies favored by business. Thus, whereas "in-terested" minorities in the Democratic party typically supported each other's programs, each "interested" minority in the Re-publican party stood alone. The Republican leadership re-sponded to the legislative demands of each minority by mobiliz-ing the rest of the party to oppose them. City Republicans joined colleagues from the traditional "heartland" in voting against farm bills; Farm Belt members joined members from the "heartland" in opposing housing bills; almost everyone answered the party call in voting on labor or public power questions. A Republican congressman was quite likely to be least loyal to his party in voting on issues of immediate dis-trict concern. On a good proportion of farm, city, labor, and Western roll calls, a sizable number of Republicans from "in-terested" districts found it advisable to vote with the Democrats. This pattern of "exclusive" compromise may be symbolized as follows: "E" stands for a proeconomy and probusiness attitude "whenever possible," the single "E" on the left for the attitude of Republicans from the "heartland."

$$F + E, \ C + E, \ E, \ L + E, \ W + E \ \rightarrow \ E$$

A final demonstration of the positions of the four "interested" minorities in each of the congressional parties is given in Figures 26 and 27. Each of the eight curves in Figure 26 is

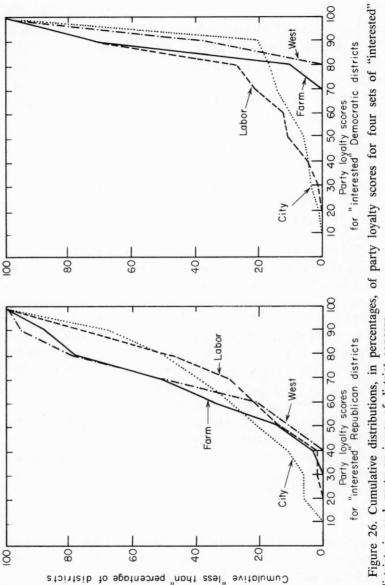

Figure 26. Cumulative distributions, in percentages, of party loyalty scores for four sets of "interested" districts in each party on issues of district concern.

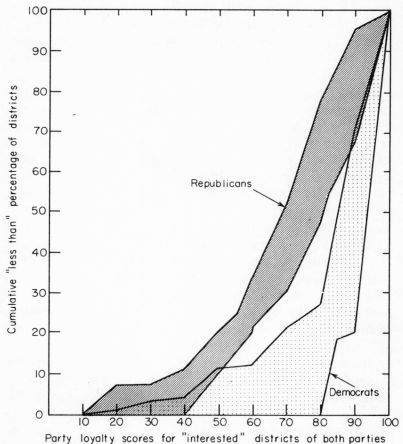

Party loyalty scores for "interested" districts of both parties

Figure 27. Superimposition of Figure 26 Democratic cumulative
party loyalty distributions on Figure 26 Republican distributions.

derived from a frequency distribution in a preceding chapter;
each is a cumulative distribution, in percentages, of party
loyalty scores for a set of "interested" districts in one party on
issues of district concern. Any point on a curve in Figure 26

gives the percentage of districts in a set with party loyalty scores less than the value indicated below on the horizontal axis. In Figure 26, the closer a curve clings to the lower right-hand corner of a graph, the higher is the range of district loyalty scores it records.

Figure 26 is, in fact, a rehearsal for the production of Figure 27. In the latter Figure, the area enclosed by the four curves of each party in Figure 26 has been shaded, and the shaded area of one party has been superimposed on the shaded area of the other. The result is a convincing proof of the difference between the two parties in their treatment of "interested" minorities. On these four sets of "bread and butter" issues, each postwar party dealt with all its minorities in a distinctive fashion. The spread, in Figure 27, between the shaded areas of the two parties reflects the difference between the policies of "exclusive" and "inclusive" compromise. The Republicans, on farm, city, labor, and Western matters, adopted policies which quite often stimulated their "interested" members to bolt party ranks. The Democrats insured party loyalty among their "interested" elements by granting minority programs official party endorsement.

It is tempting to attribute the difference in compromise formulas to a difference in party ideologies. One Republican congressman has stated the philosophical distinction in the simplest possible terms: "They tell people what they are going to do *for* them, we tell them what we are keeping the government from doing *to* them."[10] The "inclusive" approach of the Democrats manifestly facilitated the kinds of raids on the Treasury which collectively comprised the party program. The astringent Manchesterian liberalism of the Republicans was served equally well by an "exclusive" approach. It is tempting, and yet judgment must be suspended. A relevant

10. Quoted in Clapp, *The Congressman*, p. 19.

point is that the Democrats were the majority party in the nation throughout this postwar period. The Republicans had fallen into the habit of being an opposition, and neither the 1946 election nor the reluctant leadership of President Eisenhower could convince them that they were in Washington to favor things rather than oppose them. More important, the Democrats had, in the agenda of President Roosevelt, set the terms of national debate; their strategy could be "inclusive" because the dominant issues in politics rendered this course the natural and profitable one.

In fact, it may be true that "inclusive" compromise is the hallmark of a *dominant* party rather than a welfarist one, that the best way to build a majority party in America is to impress upon the electorate issues which make "inclusive" legislative practices possible. Ventures into the past are exceedingly dangerous, but it may be worth while to point to the ancient connection between the Republican party and the protective tariff. E. E. Schattschneider wrote in 1935 that "the dominant position of the Republican party before 1932 can be attributed largely to the successful exploitation of the tariff by this party as a means of attaching to itself a formidable array of interests dependent on the protective system and intent upon continuing it."[11] How were these interests welded together in Congress? "Compensatory duties are used to implement a strategy of reciprocal noninterference in which each industry is encouraged to seek duties of its own and induced to accept the incidental burdens of the system without protest."[12]

Even if raids were made on the consumer rather than on the Treasury, all this sounds very much like a successful pattern of "inclusive" compromise. For decades, with a reflexive-

11. *Politics, Pressures and the Tariff,* reprinted (Hamden, Conn., 1963), p. 283.
12. Schattschneider, p. 284.

ness devoid of reason, a Republican congressional victory heralded a general increase in the tariff rates. Democrats, like Republicans of recent years, were in the role of naysayers. The New Dealers, in handing the tariff schedule over to a commission, may have thereby torn the heart out of the Republican party. But even in the 1950's one could find occasional Pennsylvania Republicans, suggestive of the writhing limbs of a dismembered reptile, who offered higher tariffs as the only solution to the world's ills.

STABILITY AND VARIATION

To go back to the postwar years, what were the legislative results of these patterns of inclusion and exclusion? First of all, with the parties handling issues as they did, it is only logical to expect that different kinds of constituencies should have favored one party more than the other. It has been asserted that this postwar period was one of notable stability in electoral alignments, and the data in Figure 28 lend some confirmation to the claim. Figure 28 measures, for each postwar Congress, the difference between the proportion of given subsets of congressmen who were Republicans and the proportion of all congressmen who were Republicans. Thus, for example, in the Eighty-seventh Congress, 174 of 437, or 39.9 percent, of all congressmen were Republicans, and 32 of 111, or 28.8 percent, of all farm congressmen were Republicans; the point on the graph for farm members of that Congress appears eleven percentage units below the zero line.

Figure 28 shows that the Republicans, regardless of electoral swings, enjoyed proportionately about the same degree of success in each given type of congressional district throughout the postwar era. The party fared consistently worse in farm, city, and labor districts than it did in the country as a whole.

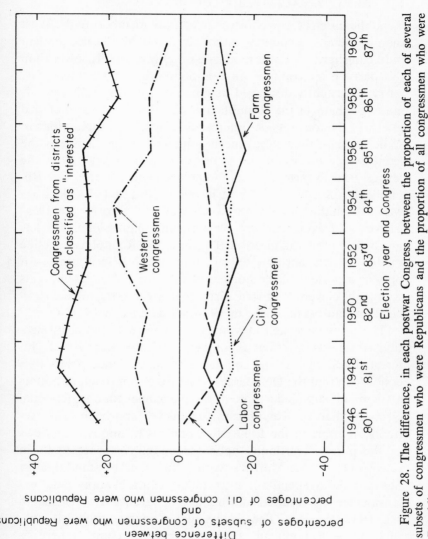

Figure 28. The difference, in each postwar Congress, between the proportion of each of several subsets of congressmen who were Republicans and the proportion of all congressmen who were Republicans.

Republicans elected proportionately more members in the West than in the entire country, although, it should be said, the Republican share of Western congressmen was usually lower than the party proportion of all non-Southern congressmen. The party consistently displayed its greatest strength in districts — many of them in the Republican "heartland" — not included in any of the four sets of "interested" districts. (Fluctuations in some of these time series merit comment. That 1948 was the leanest year for Republicans in labor districts and 1956 the leanest year in farm districts should cause no surprise. The Republican upsurge in the West in the 1952 and 1954 elections was attributable in good part to the skill of California state legislators in carving out new Republican congressional districts just before the 1952 election. The apparent Republican decline in the districts not counted as "interested" is intriguing — if only as a portent of the horrors of the mid-1960's. Democrats won only eleven Northern seats in this category in the 1948 election, but twenty-eight in 1958 and twenty in 1960.)

The problem which inevitably confronted Republican election strategists was that there were a sizable number of "interested" districts in the country. All the evidence points to a conclusion that the Democratic "inclusive" approach to minority demands supplied a more attractive banner for congressional elections than the Republican "exclusive" approach. The Republican effort in the Eightieth Congress to impose the views of the party "heartland" upon the country ("what looks in retrospect," in Joe Martin's words, "like the last stand against heavy federal spending, high taxes, centralization, and extravagance"[13]) resulted in a net loss of seventy-five districts in the 1948 election. The Eighty-first Congress included only nine fewer Republicans from districts not counted here as "interested," but thirty-three fewer Republicans from "labor

13. Martin, *My First Fifty Years in Politics*, p. 177.

districts," thirty-one fewer from "city districts," thirteen fewer from "farm districts," and seven fewer from "Western districts." (Because some districts fell into more than one "interested" category, these losses add up to more than seventy-five.) The likelihood is that, in these years, the Republican party in the House could be pure only at the cost of being small. A durable improvement in party fortunes either in the urban and industrial North or in the rural South would probably have imported into the party a good degree of heresy on one issue or another.

If the relative strength of Republicans and Democrats in different kinds of districts was fairly constant, the absolute strength of each party in the Congress was not. When the political pendulum swung, it swung in all sorts of districts, and its movements were of political consequence. The number of Democrats elected to each postwar Congress is given in Figure 29. The workings of congressional compromise, however, rendered the congressional election an exceptionally delicate instrument for translating the popular will into public policy. There was, in particular, a good deal of indirect representation. In the North, two congressmen of opposite parties from the same set of "interested" districts were more likely to agree on issues of district relevance than were two congressmen of opposite parties from districts "indifferent" on those issues. Thus to a New York voter favoring public housing an election in New York City may have been of less importance than an election in South Dakota; New York City congressmen of both parties were likely to vote for public housing but the odds were that a Democrat and a Republican from South Dakota would disagree. Similarly, a North Dakota wheat farmer should have watched the returns in New Jersey; what happened in an election in that state may have been of greater legislative consequence on wheat problems than what hap-

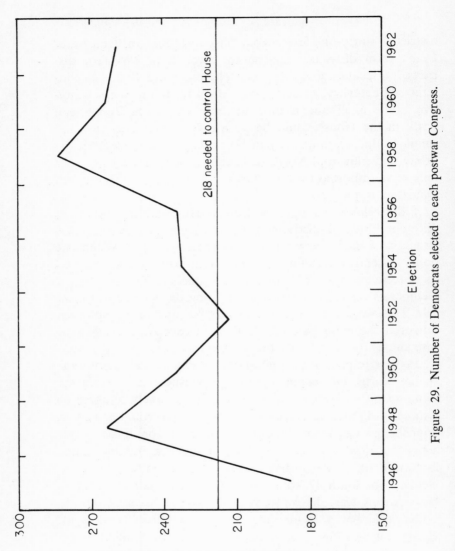

Figure 29. Number of Democrats elected to each postwar Congress.

pened. in North Dakota. Democratic and Republican congressmen from the state of Washington were inclined to agree on public power questions, but Democrats and Republicans from Michigan were not. The tendency for electoral trends to run from coast to coast, however, made a lot of sense; Democratic gains anywhere in the North aided all the elements of the party coalition, and Republican gains anywhere in the North signified that federal programs of all kinds were likely to be trimmed.

The amplitude of the pendulum swing was exceedingly important. Republicans with a slim House majority could not proceed to dismantle the federal government, and Democrats with a narrow majority could not give satisfaction to all their suppliant minorities. Of great relevance on the Democratic side was the fact that the party's "indifferent" congressmen could be mobilized more completely on some sets of issues than on others. The point is illustrated in Figure 30. Each of the four curves in the figure is derived from a frequency distribution in a previous chapter; each is a cumulative distribution, in percentages, of cohesion indices for a set of "indifferent" congressmen on issues that inspired their presumed indifference. The range of cohesion indices is rather lower for "indifferents" on labor and city issues than on farm and Western issues. In other words, more Democrats, especially Southern Democrats, voted with the Republicans on the former issues than on the latter.

The result was that the Democrats required House majorities of different sizes in order to gratify their different minorities. When the party gained or lost seats it gained or lost them in the North, and the chances were good that any Northern Democrat would loyally participate in intraparty logrolling. On farm policy, the party lost control of the House only in the Republican Eightieth and Eighty-third Congresses. With the

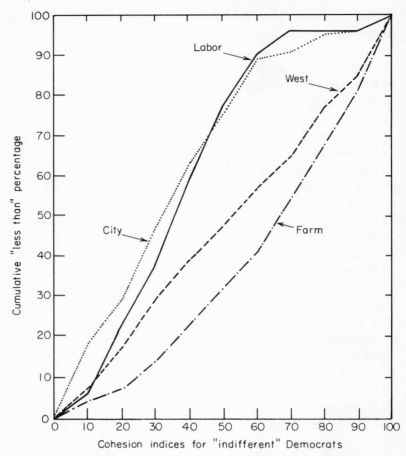

Figure 30. Cumulative distributions, in percentages, of cohesion indices for four sets of "indifferent" Democratic congressmen on issues on which they were "indifferent."

support of a number of farm bloc Republicans, and with the customary backing of city and industrial Democrats, party leaders needed a party membership of only about 230 to protect or shepherd through Congress Democratic farm programs. With the evaporation of Republican support in the late 1950's, the requirement rose to about 260.

On city and labor issues, however, 230 Democrats were never enough; more Northern members were needed to cancel out Southern defectors. Substantial housing bills were passed only in the Eighty-first, Eighty-sixth, and Eighty-seventh Congresses, all of them with Democratic memberships of over 260. When, in the 1951–1958 period, the Democratic share of House seats fell below 240, the public housing program enacted in 1949 was decimated by Southern Democrats and Republicans. (The 260 figure seems to have been critical in another area. When Democrats numbered 260 or more, party leaders possessed the necessary resources to challenge the power of the Rules Committee. Hence the establishment of the 21-day rule in the Eighty-first Congress, its abolishment in the Eighty-second, and the "packing" of the Committee in the Eighty-seventh Congress after Rules "promises" to report out liberal legislation had not been fulfilled in the Eighty-sixth.) The breaking-point on the thornier labor questions — minimum wage and labor-management relations — lay well above the 280 mark. Never in these years did labor interests have the upper hand in the House. It is worthy of note that 322 Democrats were elected to the Congress that passed the Wagner Act in 1935, and that 333 Democratic Representatives sat in the Congress that enacted — narrowly — the Fair Labor Standards Act in 1938.

The 1964 election, of course, unleashed all the Democratic minorities and permitted them to enact into law the schemes of an entire generation. Spokesmen for Westerners, for city dwellers, for farmers, even for labor — all of them could flourish in a House harboring 294 Democrats. The Republicans sat helplessly by, and President Johnson was able to enhance his reputation as a legislative wizard. Here was "inclusive" compromise with enough participants to make benefits available to everyone. There were signs in 1965, moreover, that this Johnsonian coalition might be stabilized at somewhere near its peak level of efficiency. The Supreme Court had decided in 1962 and 1964 that legislators, state and national, ought to represent people rather than anything else. More important were the changes in the South; the federal government resolved in 1965 to extend the suffrage to Southern Negroes. In a sense the nation, having opted for social democracy in the North decades earlier, was now choosing to drop the other shoe.

But the politics of the immediate postwar period were, as Samuel Lubell has described them, a politics of stalemate.[14] In the 1947–1962 period the Democrats were, to be sure, the majority party in the country. The triumph of the New Deal had been a triumph for welfare state philosophy, for the notion that government exists to distribute loaves and fishes rather than to protect private property. The postwar Democratic party was the offspring of the New Deal, and it must be said that "inclusive" compromise — the pattern of intraparty accommodation adopted by postwar Democrats in the House — was in principle an excellent mechanism for distributing loaves and fishes. Fortunately or unfortunately, however, the goods in these years were not handed out in equal portions. Democratic congressmen from city and industrial areas kept the farm programs going, but a sizable number of Southern Democrats did not reciprocate on housing and labor issues. The more that programs favored lower income groups, the less inclined Democratic Congresses were to pass them. Postwar Congresses with normal Democratic majorities spoke dutifully in Rooseveltian language, but the welfare state they helped to construct was a conservative one indeed.

14. *The Future of American Politics,* 2nd ed. (Garden City, N.Y., 1956).

BIBLIOGRAPHY/INDEX

BIBLIOGRAPHY

The *Congressional Record,* 1947–1962, and the *Congressional Quarterly Almanac* and/or *Congressional Quarterly Weekly Report,* also 1947–1962, were by far the most important sources in this study. Almost all the other sources listed below were used in surveying the field of congressional voting analysis or in tracing postwar policy developments on relevant domestic issues.

Aaron, Benjamin. "Amending the Taft-Hartley Act: A Decade of Frustration," *Industrial and Labor Relations Review,* 11:327–338 (April 1958).

Acheson, Dean. *A Democrat Looks at His Party.* New York: Harper and Brothers, 1955.

Allen, Howard W. "Geography and Politics: Voting on Reform Issues in the United States Senate, 1911–1916," *Journal of Southern History,* 27:216–228 (May 1961).

Anderson, Lee F. "Variability in the Unidimensionality of Legislative Voting," *Journal of Politics,* 26:568–585 (August 1964).

Andrain, Charles F. "A Scale Analysis of Senators' Attitudes Toward Civil Rights," *Western Political Quarterly,* 17:488–503 (September 1964).

Andrews, Stanley. *The Farmer's Dilemma.* Washington: Public Affairs Press, 1961.

Bailey, Stephen K. *Congress Makes a Law: The Story Behind the Employment Act of 1946.* New York: Columbia University Press, 1950.

Belknap, George M. "A Method for Analyzing Legislative Behavior," *Midwest Journal of Political Science,* 2:377–402 (November 1958).

Benedict, Murray R. *Farm Policies of the United States, 1790–1950: A Study of Their Origins and Development.* New York: Twentieth Century Fund, 1953.

Berdahl, Clarence A. "Some Notes on Party Membership in Congress," *American Political Science Review,* 43:309–321 (April 1949); 492–508 (June 1949); 721–734 (August 1949).

Beyer, Glenn H. *Housing: A Factual Analysis.* New York: Macmillan, 1958.

Beyle, Herman C. *Identification and Analysis of Attribute-Cluster-Blocs.* Chicago: University of Chicago Press, 1931.

Binkley, Wilfred E. *American Political Parties: Their Natural History,* 3rd ed. New York: Alfred A. Knopf, 1959.

Black, John D. "The McNary-Haugen Movement," *American Economic Review,* 18:405–427 (September 1928).

Bolling, Richard. *House Out of Order.* New York: E. P. Dutton and Company, 1965.

Brimhall, Dean R., and Arthur S. Otis. "Consistency of Voting by Our Congressmen," *Journal of Applied Psychology,* 32:1–14 (February 1948).

Brown, Emily Clark. *National Labor Policy: Taft-Hartley After Three Years and the Next Steps.* Washington: Public Affairs Institute, Report No. 6, 1950.

Buchanan, James M., and Gordon Tullock. *The Calculus of Consent: Logical Foundations of Constitutional Democracy.* Ann Arbor: University of Michigan Press, 1962.

Christenson, Reo M. *The Brannan Plan: Farm Politics and Policy.* Ann Arbor: University of Michigan Press, 1959.

Clapp, Charles L. *The Congressman: His Work as He Sees It.* Washington: Brookings, 1963.

Connerton, Robert J. "The Practical Impact of the New Law," *Proceedings of Thirteenth Annual Meeting of Industrial Relations Research Association,* 1960, pp. 27–39.

Crane, Wilder, Jr. "A Caveat on Roll-Call Studies of Party Voting," *Midwest Journal of Political Science,* 4:237–249 (August 1960).

Dahl, Robert A. *Congress and Foreign Policy.* New York: Harcourt, Brace and Company, 1950.

de Grazia, Alfred. *The Western Public.* Stanford, Calif.: Stanford University Press, 1954.

Dempsey, Paul. "Liberalism-Conservatism and Party Loyalty in the U.S. Senate," *Journal of Social Psychology,* 56:159–170 (April 1962).

de Roos, Robert, and Arthur A. Maass, "The Lobby that Can't Be Licked," *Harper's,* August 1949, pp. 21–30.

Dexter, Lewis A. "The Representative and His District," *Human Organization,* 16:2–13 (Spring 1957).

Dummett, Michael, and Robin Farquharson. "Stability in Voting," *Econometrica,* 29:33–43 (January 1961).

Eulau, Heinz, John C. Wahlke, William Buchanan, and Leroy C. Ferguson. "The Role of the Representative: Some Empirical Observations on the Theory of Edmund Burke," *American Political Science Review,* 53:742–756 (September 1959).

Farris, Charles D. "A Method of Determining Ideological Groupings in the Congress," *Journal of Politics,* 20:308–338 (May 1958).

Fenno, Richard F., Jr. "The House Appropriations Committee as a Political System: The Problem of Integration," *American Political Science Review,* 56:310–324 (June 1962).

Fenton, John H., and Kenneth N. Vines. "Negro Registration in Louisiana," *American Political Science Review,* 51:704–713 (September 1957).

Fiellin, Alan. "The Functions of Informal Groups in Legislative Institutions," *Journal of Politics,* 24:72–91 (February 1962).

Fite, Gilbert C. *George N. Peek and the Fight for Farm Parity.* Norman: University of Oklahoma Press, 1954.

Foard, Ashley A., and Hilbert Fefferman. "Federal Urban Renewal Legislation," *Law and Contemporary Problems,* 25:635–684 (Autumn 1960).

Froman, Lewis A., Jr. "Inter-Party Constituency Differences and Congressional Voting Behavior," *American Political Science Review,* 57:57–61 (March 1963).

Gage, N. L., and Ben Shimberg. "Measuring Senatorial 'Progressivism,'" *Journal of Abnormal and Social Psychology,* 44:112–117 (January 1949).

Galloway, George B. *History of the House of Representatives.* New York: Thomas Y. Crowell Company, 1961.

——— "Leadership in the House of Representatives," *Western Political Quarterly,* 12:417–441 (June 1959).

Gamson, William A. "An Experimental Test of a Theory of Coalition Formation," *American Sociological Review,* 26:565–573 (August 1961).

Gilpatrick, Thomas V. "Price Support Policy and the Midwest Farm Vote," *Midwest Journal of Political Science,* 3:319–335 (November 1959).

Golzé, Alfred R. *Reclamation in the United States.* Caldwell, Idaho: Caxton Printers, 1961.

Goodwin, George, Jr. "The Seniority System in Congress," *American Political Science Review,* 53:412–436 (June 1959).

——— "Subcommittees: The Miniature Legislatures of Congress," *American Political Science Review,* 56:596–604 (September 1962).

Grassmuck, George L. *Sectional Biases in Congress on Foreign Policy.* Baltimore: Johns Hopkins Press, 1951.

Griffith, Ernest S. *Congress, Its Contemporary Role,* 3rd ed. New York: New York University Press, 1961.

Gross, Bertram. *The Legislative Struggle: A Study in Social Combat.* New York: McGraw-Hill, 1953.

Grumm, John G. "A Factor Analysis of Legislative Behavior," *Midwest Journal of Political Science,* 7:336–356 (November 1963).

——— "The Systematic Analysis of Blocs in the Study of Legislative Behavior," *Western Political Quarterly,* 18:350–362 (June 1965).

Halloway, Harry. "The Negro and the Vote: The Case of Texas," *Journal of Politics,* 23:526–556 (August 1961).

Hardin, Charles M. "The Politics of Agriculture in the United States," *Journal of Farm Economics,* 32:571–583 (November 1950).

——— "The Republican Department of Agriculture: A Political Interpretation," *Journal of Farm Economics,* 36:210–227 (May 1954).

——— "Farm Price Policy and the Farm Vote," *Journal of Farm Economics,* 37:601–624 (November 1955).

Harris, Chester W. "A Factor Analysis of Selected Senate Roll Calls, 80th Congress," *Educational and Psychological Measurement,* 8:583–591 (Winter 1948).

Hartman, George W., and John C. Hook. "Substandard Urban Housing in the United States: A Quantitative Analysis," in Harold M. Mayer and Clyde F. Kohn, eds. *Readings in Urban Geography.* Chicago: University of Chicago Press, 1959, pp. 511–529.

Hathaway, Dale E., and Lawrence W. Witt. "Agricultural Policy: Whose Valuations?" *Journal of Farm Economics,* 34:299–309 (August 1952).

Haystead, Ladd, and Gilbert C. Fite. *The Agricultural Regions of the United States.* Norman: University of Oklahoma Press, 1955.

Heinz, Jack. "Those Annoying Farmers: Impossible But Not Really Serious," *Harper's,* July 1963, pp. 61–68.

Hirschman, Albert O. *Journeys Toward Progress.* New York: Twentieth Century Fund, 1963.

Holcombe, Arthur N. *The Political Parties of To-Day,* 2nd ed. New York: Harper and Brothers, 1925.

Hughes, Emmet J. *The Ordeal of Power: A Political Memoir of the Eisenhower Years.* New York: Atheneum, 1963.

Huntington, Samuel P. "A Revised Theory of American Politics," *American Political Science Review,* 44:669–677 (September 1950).

Jewell, Malcolm E. *Senatorial Politics and Foreign Policy.* Lexington, Ky.: University of Kentucky Press, 1962.

——— "Evaluating the Decline of Southern Internationalism Through

Senatorial Roll Call Votes," *Journal of Politics,* 21:624–646 (November 1959).

Johnson, Thomas F., James R. Morris, and Joseph G. Butts. *Renewing America's Cities.* Washington: Institute for Social Science Research, 1962.

Jonas, Frank H., ed. *Western Politics.* Salt Lake City: University of Utah Press, 1961.

Jones, Charles O. "Representation in Congress: The Case of the House Agriculture Committee," *American Political Science Review,* 55:358–367 (June 1961).

———— "The Role of the Congressional Subcommittee," *Midwest Journal of Political Science,* 6:327–344 (November 1962).

Jones, William O. "Current Farm Price-Support Proposals in the United States," *Journal of Politics,* 13:253–268 (May 1951).

Kantor, Harry S. "Two Decades of the Fair Labor Standards Act." *Monthly Labor Review,* 81:1097–1106 (October 1958).

Kessel, John H. "The Washington Congressional Delegation," *Midwest Journal of Political Science,* 8:1–21 (February 1964).

Key, V. O., Jr. *Southern Politics in State and Nation.* New York: Alfred A. Knopf, 1949.

———— *A Primer of Statistics for Political Scientists.* New York: Thomas Y. Crowell Company, 1954.

———— *Public Opinion and American Democracy.* New York: Alfred A. Knopf, 1961.

Knapp, David C. "Congressional Control of Agricultural Conservation Policy: A Case Study of the Appropriations Process," *Political Science Quarterly,* 71:257–281 (June 1956).

Leek, John H. *Government and Labor in the United States.* New York: Rinehart and Company, 1952.

Lerche, Charles O., Jr. "Southern Congressmen and the 'New Isolationism,'" *Political Science Quarterly,* 75:321–337 (September 1960).

Lowell, A. Lawrence. "The Influence of Party Upon Legislation in England and America," *Annual Report of the American Historical Association for 1901,* I, 319–542. Reprinted Washington: U.S. Government Printing Office, 1902.

Lowi, Theodore. "How the Farmers Get What They Want," *Reporter,* May 21, 1964, pp. 33–38.

Lubell, Samuel. *The Future of American Politics,* 2nd ed. Garden City, N.Y.: Doubleday, 1956.

Luce, R. Duncan, and Arnold A. Rogow. "A Game Theoretic Analysis of Congressional Power Distributions for a Stable Two-Party System," *Behavioral Science,* 1:83–95 (April 1956).

Maass, Arthur. *Muddy Waters: The Army Engineers and the Nation's Rivers.* Cambridge, Mass.: Harvard University Press, 1951.
———— "Congress and Water Resources," *American Political Science Review,* 44:576–593 (September 1950).
McAdams, Alan K. *Power and Politics in Labor Legislation.* New York: Columbia University Press, 1964.
McConnell, Grant. *The Decline of Agrarian Democracy.* Berkeley and Los Angeles: University of California Press, 1953.
McDonnell, Timothy L., S.J. *The Wagner Housing Act: A Case Study of the Legislative Process.* Chicago: Loyola University Press, 1957.
MacNeil, Neil. *Forge of Democracy: The House of Representatives.* New York: David McKay Company, 1963.
MacRae, Duncan, Jr. *Dimensions of Congressional Voting: A Statistical Study of the House of Representatives in the Eighty-first Congress.* Berkeley and Los Angeles: University of California Press, 1958.
———— "The Relation Between Roll Call Votes and Constituencies in the Massachusetts House of Representatives," *American Political Science Review,* 46:1046–1055 (December 1952).
———— "Some Underlying Variables in Legislative Roll Call Votes," *Public Opinion Quarterly,* 18:191–196 (Summer 1954).
———— "Occupations and the Congressional Vote, 1940–1950," *American Sociological Review,* 20:332–340 (June 1955).
———— "Roll Call Votes and Leadership," *Public Opinion Quarterly,* 20:543–558 (Fall 1956).
MacRae, Duncan, Jr., and Hugh D. Price. "Scale Positions and 'Power' in the Senate," *Behavioral Science,* 4:212–218 (July 1959).
March, James G. "Party Legislative Representation as a Function of Election Results," *Public Opinion Quarterly,* 21:521–542 (Winter 1957).
Marshall, Ray. "Some Factors Influencing the Growth of Unions in the South," *Proceedings of Thirteenth Annual Meeting of Industrial Relations Research Association,* 1960, pp. 166–182.
Martin, Joe. *My First Fifty Years in Politics.* New York: McGraw-Hill, 1960.
Masters, Nicholas A. "Committee Assignments in the House of Representatives," *American Political Science Review,* 55:345–357 (June 1961).
Masters, Nicholas A., and Deil S. Wright. "Trends and Variations in the Two-Party Vote: The Case of Michigan," *American Political Science Review,* 52:1078–1090 (December 1958).
Matthews, Donald R., and James W. Prothro. "Social and Economic

Factors and Negro Voter Registration in the South," *American Political Science Review*, 57:24–44 (March 1963).

Meller, Norman. "Legislative Behavior Research," *Western Political Quarterly*, 13:131–153 (March 1960).

Meyerson, Martin, Barbara Terrett, and William L. C. Wheaton. *Housing, People, and Cities*. New York: McGraw-Hill, 1962.

Miller, Warren E., and Donald E. Stokes. "Constituency Influence in Congress," *American Political Science Review*, 57:45–56 (March 1963).

Moos, Malcolm, ed. *H. L. Mencken on Politics: A Carnival of Buncombe*. New York: Vintage, 1960.

Morgan, Robert J. "Pressure Politics and Resources Administration," *Journal of Politics*, 18:39–60 (February 1956).

Nieburg, N. L. "The Eisenhower AEC and Congress: A Study in Executive-Legislative Relations," *Midwest Journal of Political Science*, 6:115–148 (May 1962).

Paarlberg, Don. *American Farm Policy: A Case Study of Centralized Decision-Making*. New York: John Wiley and Sons, 1964.

Pelling, Henry. *American Labor*. Chicago: University of Chicago Press, 1960.

Pennock, J. Roland. "Party and Constituency in Postwar Agricultural Price-Support Legislation," *Journal of Politics*, 18:167–210 (May 1956).

"The Political Impasse in Farm Support Legislation," *Yale Law Journal*, 71:952–978 (April 1962).

Price, Hugh D. "Scale Analysis of Senate Voting Patterns, 1949–1956," Unpub. diss. Harvard University, 1958.

Reilly, Gerard D. "The Legislative History of the Taft-Hartley Act," *George Washington Law Review*, 29:285–300 (December 1960).

Review of Federal Housing Programs, appendix to Senate Committee on Banking and Currency, 87th Congress, 1st Session, *Hearings on Various Bills to Amend the Federal Housing Laws*.

Rice, Stuart A. *Quantitative Methods in Politics*. New York: Alfred A. Knopf, 1928.

——— "The Behavior of Legislative Groups: A Method of Measurement," *Political Science Quarterly*, 40:60–72 (March 1925).

Ridgeway, Marian E. *The Missouri Basin's Pick-Sloan Plan: A Case Study in Congressional Policy Determination*. Urbana, Ill.: University of Illinois Press, 1955.

Rieselbach, Leroy N. "The Basis of Isolationist Behavior," *Public Opinion Quarterly*, 24:645–657 (Winter 1960).

——— "The Demography of the Congressional Vote on Foreign Aid,

1939–1958," *American Political Science Review,* 58:577–588 (September 1964).

Riker, William H. "The Paradox of Voting and Congressional Rules for Voting on Amendments," *American Political Science Review,* 52:349–366 (June 1958).

———— "A Method for Determining the Significance of Roll Calls in Voting Bodies," in John Wahlke and Heinz Eulau, eds., *Legislative Behavior: A Reader in Theory and Research* (Glencoe, Ill.: Free Press, 1959), pp. 377–384.

Riker, William H., and Donald Niemi. "The Stability of Coalitions on Roll Calls in the House of Representatives," *American Political Science Review,* 56:58–65 (March 1962).

Ripley, Randall B. "The Party Whip Organizations in the United States House of Representatives," *American Political Science Review,* 58:561–576 (September 1964).

Roach, Hannah. "Sectionalism in Congress (1870 to 1900)," *American Political Science Review,* 19:500–526 (August 1925).

Robinson, James A. *Congress and Foreign Policy-Making: A Study in Legislative Influence and Initiative.* Homewood, Illinois: Dorsey Press, 1962.

Rustow, Dankwart A. *The Politics of Compromise: A Study of Parties and Cabinet Government in Sweden.* Princeton: Princeton University Press, 1955.

Schattschneider, E. E. *Politics, Pressures and the Tariff.* Hamden, Conn.: Archon Books, 1963.

Shils, Edward B. "The Impact of Landrum-Griffin on the Small Employer," *Annals of the American Academy of Political and Social Science,* 333:141–152 (January 1961).

Shister, Joseph. "The Impact of the Taft-Hartley Act on Union Strength and Collective Bargaining," *Industrial and Labor Relations Review,* 11:339–351 (April 1958).

Smith, Frank E. *Congressman from Mississippi.* New York: Random House, 1964.

Soth, Lauren. *Farm Trouble.* Princeton: Princeton University Press, 1957.

Stokes, Donald E., and Warren E. Miller. "Party Government and the Saliency of Congress," *Public Opinion Quarterly,* 26:531–546 (Winter 1962).

Taft, Philip. "The Impact of Landrum-Griffin on Union Government," *Annals of the American Academy of Political and Social Science,* 333:130–140 (January 1961).

Talbot, Ross B. "Farm Legislation in the 86th Congress," *Journal of Farm Economics,* 43:582–605 (August 1961).

Troy, Leo. *Distribution of Union Membership among the States: 1939 and 1953*. Occasional Paper 56. New York: National Bureau of Economic Research Inc., 1957.

Truman, David B. *The Congressional Party: A Case Study*. New York: John Wiley and Sons, 1959.

———— "The State Delegations and the Structure of Party Voting in the U.S. House of Representatives," *American Political Science Review*, 50:1023–1045 (December 1956).

Turner, Julius. *Party and Constituency: Pressures on Congress*. Baltimore: Johns Hopkins Press, 1951.

Tyler, Gus. *A Legislative Campaign for a Federal Minimum Wage (1955)*. New York: Henry Holt and Company, Eagleton Case Study, 1959.

U.S. Bureau of the Census. *Congressional District Data Book, Districts of the 87th Congress*, 1961.

U.S. Bureau of the Census. *U.S. Census of Agriculture: 1950*, vol I, Counties and State Economic Areas.

U.S. Bureau of the Census. *U.S. Census of Population: 1950*, vol III, Characteristics of the Population.

Urich, Theodore. "The Voting Behavior of Freshmen Congressmen," *Southwestern Social Science Quarterly*, 39:337–341 (March 1959).

Van Camp, John. "What Happened to the Labor-Reform Bill?" *Reporter*, October 2, 1958, pp. 24–28.

Wahlke,, John C., and Heinz Eulau, eds. *Legislative Behavior: A Reader in Theory and Research*. Glencoe, Ill.: Free Press, 1959.

Watson, Richard A. "The Tariff Revolution: A Study of Shifting Party Attitudes," *Journal of Politics*, 18:678–701 (November 1956).

Weiss, Harry. "Economic Effects of a Nationwide Minimum Wage," *Proceedings of Ninth Annual Meeting of Industrial Relations Research Association*, 1956, pp. 154–166.

Wengert, Norman. *Natural Resources and the Political Struggle*. Garden City, N.Y.: Doubleday and Company, 1955.

Westerfield, H. Bradford. *Foreign Policy and Party Politics: Pearl Harbor to Korea*. New Haven: Yale University Press, 1955.

White, William S. *Home Place: The Story of the U.S. House of Representatives*. Boston: Houghton-Mifflin, 1965.

Williams, Albert N. *The Water and the Power: Development of the Five Great Rivers of the West*. New York: Duell, Sloan, and Pearce, 1951.

INDEX

HARVARD POLITICAL STUDIES

* Out of print

John Fairfield Sly. *Town Government in Massachusetts* (*1620– 1930*). 1930.*

Hugh Langdon Elsbree. *Interstate Transmission of Electric Power.* 1931.*

Benjamin Fletcher Wright, Jr. *American Interpretations of Natural Law.* 1931.*

Payson S. Wild, Jr. *Sanctions and Treaty Enforcement.* 1934.*

William P. Maddox. *Foreign Relations in British Labour Politics.* 1934.*

George C. S. Benson. *Administration of the Civil Service in Massachusetts.* 1935.*

Merle Fainsod. *International Socialism and the World War.* 1935.*

John Day Larkin. *The President's Control of the Tariff.* 1936.

E. Pendleton Herring. *Federal Commissioners.* 1936.*

John Thurston. *Government Proprietary Corporations in the English-Speaking Countries.* 1937.*

Mario Einaudi. *The Physiocratic Doctrine of Judicial Control.* 1938.

Frederick Mundell Watkins. *The Failure of Constitutional Emergency Powers under the German Republic.* 1939.*

G. Griffith Johnson, Jr., *The Treasury and Monetary Policy, 1933– 1938.* 1939.*

Arnold Brecht and Comstock Glaser. *The Art and Technique of Administration in German Ministries.* 1940.*

Oliver Garceau. *The Political Life of the American Medical Association.* 1941.*

Ralph F. Bischoff. *Nazi Conquest through German Culture.* 1942.*

Charles R. Cherington. *The Regulation of Railroad Abandonments.* 1948.

Samuel H. Beer. *The City of Reason.* 1949.*

Herman Miles Somers. *Presidential Agency: The Office of War Mobilization and Reconversion.* 1950.*

Adam B. Ulam. *Philosophical Foundations of English Socialism.* 1951.*

Morton Robert Godine. *The Labor Problem in the Public Service.* 1951.*

Arthur Maass. *Muddy Waters: The Army Engineers and the Nation's Rivers.* 1951.

Robert Green McCloskey. *American Conservatism in the Age of Enterprise.* 1951.*

Inis L. Claude, Jr. *National Minorities: An International Problem.* 1955.*

Joseph Cornwall Palamountain, Jr. *The Politics of Distribution.* 1955.*

Herbert J. Spiro. *The Politics of German Codetermination.* 1958.*

Harry Eckstein. *The English Health Service.* 1958.

Richard F. Fenno, Jr. *The President's Cabinet.* 1959.

Nadav Safran. *Egypt in Search of Political Community.* 1961.

Paul E. Sigmund. *Nicholas of Cusa and Medieval Political Thought.* 1963.

Sanford A. Lakoff. *Equality in Political Philosophy.* 1964.

Charles T. Goodsell. *Administration of a Revolution.* 1965.

Martha Derthick. *The National Guard in Politics.* 1965.

Bruce L. R. Smith. *The RAND Corporation: Case Study of a Nonprofit Advisory Corporation.* 1966.

David R. Mayhew. *Party Loyalty among Congressmen: The Difference between Democrats and Republicans, 1947–1962.* 1966.

Date Due